BUILDING A HIGHLY EFFECTIVE
INTELLIGENCE CAPABILITY THAT
DELIVERS VALUE AND IMPACT

The CI-Driven CEO

A LITTLE LEADERSHIP STORY
ABOUT A POWERFUL
COMPETITIVE INTELLIGENCE IDEA

GARY D. MAAG AND **DAVID J. KALINOWSKI**

ISBN 13: 978-1-957651-12-5
Library of Congress Control Number: 2022905795

Designed by: Steven Plummer, SPBookDesign.com

INDIE BOOKS INTERNATIONAL*, INC.
2424 VISTA WAY, SUITE 316
OCEANSIDE, CA 92054
www.indiebooksintl.com

CONTENTS

PREFACE

*Change is the law of life. And those who look only to
the past or present are certain to miss the future.*
—John F. Kennedy, Address in the Assembly Hall at
the Paulskirche in Frankfurt, Germany, June 25, 1963

So your company has a crack market research department and you've made a significant investment in data tools and infrastructure. Then why is it the intelligence that you gather doesn't have a direct, effective impact on your decision-making process?

The answer is simple: the intelligence you generate through traditional methods can only tell you what your competitors have done and what they're currently doing. It's nice to know, but not *need to know* because it's firmly rooted in the past and present. And as President Kennedy noted, that's a clear indication that your company is certain to miss the future.

The great news is: *you don't have to.*

Competitive Intelligence (CI) is a mature, legal, and ethical established business process, grounded in guidelines and best practices that have been tried and tested by leading CI practitioners over the past *forty years*. And it's the only such tool that can take your business out of the data-darkness of the past and present and shine a guiding light toward the future.

As we've learned over the past three decades working in the industry, CI done right can truly help any business by providing real, actionable intelligence that's simply not available through any other means. What's shocking is, after all these years and all the progress in Competitive Intelligence, many in the business world, especially those that don't really understand CI, are still convinced CI is just a kinder, gentler name for corporate spying. Nothing could be further from the truth! We know some in the CI space who think nobody still equates CI with espionage and that this perception died back in the 1990s. We wish that were true, but for many it hasn't, though the perception of CI has gotten better. It's time once and for all that we get business leaders to stop thinking "competitive intelligence" has any negative connotations and involves cloak and dagger methods.

Think about it: should accounting be viewed as a pariah because an alarming number of organizations have cooked the books? Should marketing and advertising be completely ignored because countless organizations have been less than honest about their products and services, sometimes with drastic results? Of course not. It's not the functions themselves that are the problem, but rather the people within those functions who choose to ignore legal and ethical standards.

It's the same for Competitive Intelligence. It's an absolutely essential function that actually helps identify opportunities and *reduce* risk by uncovering critical insights senior executives can use to improve decision making.

As Jack Turner learned, not only is there nothing to be afraid of when it comes to CI, it can become a transformative function when it's championed throughout an organization.

So stop thinking of Competitive Intelligence as something that's done in the shadows. It's well past time your organization embraced

CI as an essential and required discipline that fostered strategic differentiation and started looking to the future.

The target audience of this book is broad: CI researchers, analysts, and managers of CI functions seeking to build or enhance a CI function; any end-stakeholder in strategy, sales, marketing, innovation, finance, operations, and a host of other disciplines that use intelligence and want to better understand the field; senior leadership learning to embrace how a critical understanding of the external environment through insightful analysis linked to strategy will make for better investment decisions; and students seeking to learn the ways in which CI can add value and impact as they enter the business world.

PART ONE

The Unpredictable

1

THE BLACK SWAN

Jack Turner knew that, long after he retired and transformed himself into a snowbird in Florida to escape the brutal Chicago winters, he would tell this story. He would begin to spin this yarn as so many other memorable tales about life-changing events are conveyed: "I'll never forget where I was the day when ..."

Just as Jack would never forget precisely where he was the morning he first heard that Howard Hewitt, founder and patriarch of Hewitt Games, had died—riding the Green Line on the L, eastbound, coffee in one hand, *Wall Street Journal* in the other, on his way into the office while sitting across from a man who was wearing the *exact* same shoes—he would never, ever forget this moment. Boston, just around the corner from the Green Monster at Fenway Park, on campus at Boston University, dropping his son Cody off for his freshman year at college.

The dorm room made coat closets look positively luxurious. Sofia ran an impressively quick mental calculation to determine the square-footage-to-dollar cost based on the semester's lofty tuition. The horror. Cody quipped that at least he would save money on a cleaner. Jack burst out laughing at the absurdity just as his cell rang once, then stopped for a beat before a second call followed. The Andy Barrows ring.

"Andy! Remember that forced-triple we had in our sophomore year at Northwestern? Cavernous compared to the size of the dorm room my son will call home for the next year and—"

"Black swan, Jack. We are under attack from the biggest, baddest black swan our industry has ever seen, and it is real, and it is happening!"

Jack dropped the overstuffed cardboard box he had just lugged up three flights. "Andy, we just drove fifteen hours from Chicago to Boston to discover my son will have to sleep standing up at a school that's costing us roughly the GDP of Sudan. Please, cut to the chase."

"Right, um, a *New York Times* best-seller from the early aughts by an old options trader, talked about unpredictable events, something no one thinks could happen, actually happening, a.k.a. The Black Swan Event. A black swan? Swans are supposed to be white!"

"Sorry, Andy, tired man in a tiny room that's priced like a suite on the Magnificent Mile. I know what a Black Swan Event is. In fact, I believe I gave you a copy of Professor Taleb's 2001 book, *Fooled by Randomness*. Now, please, just tell me what happened?"

Jack could hear Andy breathe in deeply and exhale slowly. Repeat. "Apricus is about to announce a major entry into the games market. Our market. Word came straight from your CI team, someone tapping into your department's network of journalists."

Jack felt the claustrophobic walls closing in. Apricus dominated global e-commerce and its already massive coffers swelled when locked-down residents ordered nearly everything online throughout last year's Covid-19 pandemic. For months, speculation had swirled that Apricus was about to make a major acquisition—a nose-diving movie theater chain, a surging digital mental health care provider, maybe even a ride-share company. But an Apricus-branded entry into console gaming? The pieces didn't fit.

"Apricus? No. No way. This close to our console refresh? My team knows the supply chain inside and out. If Apricus was building a gaming console, we would have known about it ages ago. We would have seen early indicators."

Jack's response wasn't self-aggrandizing. In the decade since Jack had been named Chief Competitive Officer at Hewitt Games, he had built the company's competitive intelligence program from the ground up, taking a hands-on role in everything from recruitment and training of his team to the forging of an industry-wide, global intelligence network. That intelligence network was strongest within the vast supply chain responsible for the many components in gaming consoles and accessories. Apricus, even if they approached a console project with the utmost secrecy, simply could not tap into that supply chain without Jack hearing about it.

"That's just it, Jack. No concrete details as of yet, but word is Apricus isn't building a video game console. They're supposedly introducing an entirely new technology with the potential to make traditional video game consoles like ours obsolete. A literal game-changer."

The blind spot.

The realization made Jack's heart bounce. If there was a flaw in Hewitt's CI program, it was the fact that it was laser-focused on the direct competition: Sampson Electronics, the industry's number-two console maker, and Kenshin Entertainment, a distant third. Thanks to the long-term attractiveness of the booming $160 billion global gaming market, the threat of a new entry was always high. But leadership at Hewitt believed barriers to entry were high enough that it wouldn't face a new competitive threat. For years, Jack had pushed to break Hewitt's CI program out of its closed-off silo and into a collaborative, organization-wide entity to better detect signals of these new market entrants. The pitch he'd made to the C-suite was clear and concise: *It's* competitive *intelligence, not* competitor *intelligence. Our singular focus on the competition has created a blind spot, and if we don't broaden our focus by expanding our CI program, we risk disaster from something we're simply not looking for.*

Jack's phone shook and hummed in his ear with alerts, texts, emails, and messages. He thought of the long list of team members and C-suite executives he needed to speak with immediately, if not sooner. Suddenly the thought of staying in this child-sized dorm room for the foreseeable future—with his cell phone off—seemed appealing. He noticed a photo taped on the far wall to the right of the lone window. A grinning selfie evidently left by the former tenant, a word-bubble drawn from his lips with a message of encouragement: *You can do BIG things in small spaces!*

"Jack?" Andy Barrows.

"Honey?" Sofia.

"Dad?" Cody.

He replied to them all, but not to any of them in particular: "The black swan has landed. It's time to go to work."

2

FALLOUT

AUTUMN'S AMBER LEAVES tumbled around Jack Turner as he jogged the paved trail through Chicago's picturesque Grant Park, his worn Adidas sneakers providing a rhythmic beat. These sights, the sounds, his blood pumping; typically this was Jack's daily five-mile moment of Zen. Typically.

Life had been anything *but* typical since the world learned of Apricus entering the gaming space nearly one month ago. And what an entrance it was.

Sovereign—the not-so-subtly named product—was, in essence, software as a service for gaming. Sign up for Sovereign for a small monthly fee, and gamers would gain unlimited access to a library of Triple-A (AAA) titles, a classification to signify high-budget, high-profile games usually made and distributed by huge, well-known publishers, just about anywhere there was an Internet connection. PC, laptop, or mobile via web browser? No problem! On the couch in front of the TV? As long as you had one of Apricus' thumb-drive-sized streaming devices—inexpensive sticks that were already among the top sellers in the category—you could pick up right where you'd left off on your laptop. No problem! And it would all reportedly be delivered at the highest console standards: up to 4K resolution at sixty frames per second and with minimal latency—the bellwether for smooth, unblurred images in even the most frenetic games.

A handful of startups had attempted to bring gaming to the cloud in the past, and Hewitt itself even explored the technology for a time. They'd all crashed and burned. No one could crack the code and reliably deliver a console-quality gaming experience in the cloud—especially not at any kind of scale. Until now.

The product itself sounded impressive enough. That it was backed by Apricus's deep pockets and industry-leading global data centers made everyone at Hewitt fear a potential knockout. Why pay upward of six-hundred dollars for Hewitt's upcoming new console when you could play many of the *exact same games*, at the same quality, just about anywhere—without being tethered to a clunky box?

The bell hadn't quite tolled for Hewitt Games and the world of console gaming, but Jack envisioned the bruiser responsible for ringing the bell spitting into his hands and clapping them together, eager to yank the rope.

"Jack?" The question came from his wireless earbud. "Did you have anything you wanted to add?"

Another emergency meeting at a moment's notice. They'd been common the past month as Hewitt's C-suite tried to work the problem in a twenty-four-seven, all-hands-on-deck fashion. CEO Susan Wright had performed admirably up to this point, but these frequent calls from other executives—increasingly slapdash—had quickly become overwhelming. Jack had little doubt a meeting to discuss the volume and quality of meetings was just around the bend.

"Not at the moment. I'll have the relevant intelligence by the end of the week."

The call ended as Jack cut past the Buckingham Fountain, close enough to feel the refreshing spray. He checked his smartwatch for the time and saw a notice for the Hewitt ticker: down another 2 percent in pre-market. Hewitt Games, longtime Wall Street darling, now a favorite of vulturous short sellers. Since Apricus's reveal, Hewitt's stock was being absolutely hammered. Analysts were equally ruthless with their ratings, downgrading Hewitt Games to the sell pile with a price target that would have been considered laughable just four weeks before.

Jack's phone rang as he approached the solemn Lincoln statue. He saw the caller ID and stopped to take the call under Abe's unblinking gaze.

"Sorry to bother you with yet another call, Jack," Susan Wright launched in, calling immediately after a meeting in which they had both participated. Jack's stomach tightened.

"No problem. How can I help?"

"When you get in this morning, can you swing by my office first thing?"

"Will do, boss." Jack attempted to answer with confidence, feeling anything but. "Need me to bring anything?"

"Just you. Won't take long. See you in a bit."

The call ended. Now Jack envisioned a very different kind of bell-ringer. The bruiser was gone, and in his place stood Susan Wright, ready to toll the bell for Jack Turner.

Jack had showered on a quick trip home before heading into the office and hustling up to Hewitt Games headquarters on the forty-second floor. He couldn't tell if his hair was still damp from the water or from his own sweat.

"I plan on announcing my resignation at the end of the week," Susan Wright deadpanned, leaning back against her wide mahogany desk, the near-constant furrow in her brow looking especially deep this morning. "You're resigning?" The shock of the news coupled with relief that his own neck wasn't on the chopping block—at least not yet—made Jack feel weightless.

"I fully accept responsibility for the past month, the fact that Apricus— of all companies—could pull off something like Sovereign right under our noses. You came to me multiple times over the years, warning us we were vulnerable to just this sort of attack. 'Competitive intelligence, not *competitor* intelligence'—isn't that what you said? You repeatedly told me we have to look out for non-traditional new entrants."

Jack nodded and sighed, slumping back in his seat.

"I should have trusted my instincts, and yours, and listened to you. I didn't. Instead, I let my ego get in the way, something Howard Hewitt would have never done. Now, the board, the shareholders, the financial media—everyone wants a scapegoat. I'm giving them one."

"But Susan, you're a terrific CEO, a great leader. If anyone can get Hewitt Games through this, it's you," Jack replied, meaning every syllable.

"Thank you, Jack. That means a lot to hear you say that, but my decision is made." She stood straight and began to pace. "I'm telling you this because I'm just one part of a big shakeup that's coming to Hewitt, a shakeup that goes all the way to the top with the board of directors." She paused, collecting her thoughts. "I'm guessing you know who Ryan Corbin is?"

Jack instantly envisioned the old *Forbes* magazine cover featuring Corbin literally standing on his head. The young, high-flying entrepreneur had come out of nowhere in the late 2000s with a startup e-commerce company focused on toy sales. Somehow, someway, in just five years, Corbin made Funporium the biggest online toy-seller in the world, topping even the king of e-commerce, Apricus, in the segment.

"Of course, Corbin is a legend," Jack said. "The Can't-Miss Kid. But he's been out of the game for years since he sold his company for what, three-point-three billion?"

"Three-point-five," Susan responded, nodding. "At the time the biggest e-commerce acquisition in history. And since the day he rode off into the sunset with his billions, he's been getting outrageous offers from the biggest and best companies in the world. He turned them all down, just couldn't find the project that got his entrepreneurial juices flowing," Susan exhaled and dropped into her office chair. "Until now."

"Now? As in, Hewitt Games now?"

"Now, as in any minute the news will break that Corbin's investment firm has acquired a roughly 10 percent stake in Hewitt, and with it, an eventual seat on the board for Ryan."

Jack's already heaving emotions pinballed between excitement, fear, and sadness. Susan Wright was leaving, but Ryan Corbin was coming in? Madness!

"I take it this reformed board will also name Corbin as interim CEO?" Jack asked.

"I thought the same, but Corbin has other ideas. We spoke at length last night. Not what I expected at all." Susan smiled and gazed out the floor-to-ceiling windows over the Chicago skyline. "He is very interested in competitive intelligence, Jack. Very interested in speaking with you."

"Me?"

"Who else? It was you who led the CI-charge to help fend off the last major attack from Sampson Electronics. Ryan Corbin wants to know what CI can do to help fend off this latest attack by Apricus. He wants to understand what insights CI can provide to help formulate a new strategy and support key tactical initiatives."

Now it was Jack's turn to stand and pace. "You give me too much credit. And Sampson Electronics is no Apricus."

"I'll leave you and Ryan to discuss the details," Susan said, leaning forward, the deep forehead furrow now firmly back in place. "But know this, Jack: Ryan Corbin is a shark. Do not let his easy demeanor fool you. He beat Apricus at its own game because he saw an opening and he pounced on it. Then what did he do? He took the money and ran, left the company he started, the people he hand-picked, his family. His *baby*."

She stood and leaned forward, her palms planted firmly on her desk. "I hope his intentions for Hewitt Games are good. I really do. But I've also been in the cutthroat corporate world for too long to simply believe it. If there is one thing I want you to take from this conversation, it's this: Ryan Corbin is always two steps ahead and he never reveals his hand. Watch your back, Jack. Good or bad, you probably won't know what he's really up to until it's too late."

3

SURPRISE

SITTING WITH HIS wife on the back patio beneath the stars, as the fire pit crackled, Jack marveled at the moment. His job, his entire career, focused on looking forward, in using competitive intelligence to find the puzzle pieces of information scattered in the present and putting them all together to create a clear picture of what could happen in the future.

Yet here, now, with his wife in his arms and the stars twinkling above, with Apricus suddenly a competitor, and entrepreneur extraordinaire Ryan Corbin buying into Hewitt Games, Jack didn't have the foggiest idea what was coming next. He considered visiting an astrologer to see what all these stars had to say about it.

"You're quiet," Jack mused. "Anxious Sofia is chatty Sofia. Why are you so calm after everything I just told you?"

"Full circle, I suppose," Sofia answered. "The feeling that we've been here before, and no matter what we do, no matter how well-prepared we think we are, we'll most likely be here again."

"Oomph, you sound more like your glass-half-empty sister." Jack laughed.

"Hey, leave my sister out of this," Sofia retorted with a not-too-playful punch to Jack's shoulder. "And let me finish. We'll most likely be here again, sure, but we'll be here with the knowledge we got through it the last time and came out even better than before. We did it once; we'll do it again. And then again if we have to, getting even more knowledge and experience with every cycle."

"That's the girl I married," Jack said, planting a kiss on Sofia's cheek. "'The world breaks everyone and afterward many are strong at the broken places.'"

"My favorite Hemingway quote."

"Mine too, but that's only the first part of the quote," Jack sighed. "And that's the part that worries me about all this: the unbreakable Hewitt Games, now with the unbreakable Ryan Corbin on board."

"Worries you? Doesn't sound so bad to me. Remind me what the second part of the Hemingway quote is?"

"'The world breaks everyone and afterward many are strong at the broken places. But those that will not break'"—Jack paused—"'it kills.'"

~

The following afternoon, Jack smiled as he walked up North Rush, thankful to see the buzz of activity back in downtown Chicago post-Covid. His smile grew wider as he turned into Gibson's, the old-school steakhouse that Hewitt's original CI leader Bob Laurence adored.

Seated in his typical tufted-back booth in the rear, Laurence grinned when he saw Jack enter. Another man with dark hair sat facing Laurence, his back to Jack. But as he turned, Jack's eyes grew wide.

"Jack Turner, meet Ryan Corbin," Laurence announced as he rose. "Ryan, Jack."

Jack's first thought: *he looks fresh-out-of-B-school young.*

"Pleasure, Jack. Bob has been talking about you so much; I feel like we've already met."

"Ryan, what a surprise!" A slight build, but a vice-grip handshake.

"I wish Bob had been as forthcoming with me. I didn't know you'd be joining us today."

"Surprise!" Laurence said, with his trademark boom of a laugh, as they took their seats.

"My idea, apologies," Corbin smiled, flashing brilliant white teeth. "I wanted our initial meeting to be fresh. Might sound odd, but I've found that people often feel they need to prepare in some way when they learn they'll be sitting down with me for the first time."

Not so odd, Jack thought. *I would have spent a sleepless night in front of my computer if I'd known we'd be sitting across from each other today.*

"Color me unprepared," Jack replied with an honest laugh. "Bob, you've certainly elevated your social game. How is it, in all the years I've known you, you never once mentioned you know Ryan Corbin?"

"Me and Ryan? We go way back," Laurence said as he looked at his watch. "Twenty-two minutes way back to be exact."

"Unprepared and confused," Jack admitted. "So tell me, how is it we're all sitting here together?"

The waiter politely interrupted and took their drink order.

"I suppose it was Sampson Electronics," Corbin recalled as the waiter departed. "When word of Apricus's plunge into gaming broke and Hewitt's stock started to crash, I got a sense of *déjà vu*. Reminded me of what happened back in 2012 when Sampson pounced after Howard Hewitt died, rolling out their disk drive add-on to make gaming consoles into HD movie-players—Reel HD I believe they called it?"

"That's the one," Laurence agreed. "With two E's, like a movie reel."

"Clever name," Corbin replied. "So, I dug in, did the research, and learned all about the competitive intelligence campaign that helped save Hewitt Games. Susan Wright got most of the ink, but she gave credit where it was due. That led me to Jack Turner and the man who taught him CI, Bob Laurence. I found Bob was still plugging away with Proactive Worldwide, reached out, and asked if he could put this little surprise introduction together."

"Someone recently told me you were always two steps ahead," Jack marveled. "I think I'm beginning to understand what that means." Corbin just grinned in response. This time, Jack noticed the pronounced canines and remembered Susan Wright's warning: *Ryan Corbin is a shark.*

The waiter returned with a tray of drinks and, on Bob Laurence's cue, the trio made a toast to Sampson Electronics. Once the unique introduction was out of the way, Corbin cut straight to business.

"I just spent a small fortune on Hewitt stock because I believe in the product and I believe in the company," he said. "Admittedly, part of it is nostalgia. I grew up with Primo consoles and games, and I thought Howard Hewitt was a genius."

"You thought right," Laurence concurred.

"But I also know Hewitt is in a unique position," Corbin continued. "The price of the stock does not match the fundamental valuation, regardless of Apricus and cloud-gaming. Hewitt's legion of loyal gamers will remain with us *if* we absolutely delight them with the new Primo console, no matter what Sovereign can do."

It was the most refreshing comment about Hewitt that Jack had heard in the past month.

"Honestly? I feel like I just bought in at a huge discount," Corbin said with a shrug. "Check that—I *know* that I did. Much of that belief is rooted in the work that you did at Hewitt for twenty-some years, Bob, and that you've continued to do for the past decade, Jack. I believe competitive intelligence could be the key to not just getting us out of this hole, but to beating Apricus and cementing Hewitt as the king of gaming."

Jack wondered if his jaw was actually touching the floor. He'd been trying to explain and demonstrate the value of CI for so long, he didn't know how to react when someone recognized how critical it was to the success of a business. To Jack's gratitude, Bob Laurence broke the silence. "You certainly know how to make an old man feel valued!"

"From what I've learned the praise is well deserved, for you both. Just one problem. I believe CI could be the key, but I'm far from an expert." Corbin checked his watch. "I've got twenty minutes; give me an extended elevator speech. I want to know what the two of you believe are the *essential* elements of competitive intelligence." Corbin sat back. No pen or paper, he just listened.

Jack looked at his old friend and saw a familiar gleam in his eyes. Laurence said, "I give the floor to my good friend and *protégé*."

With a deep breath, Jack began, and what he told Ryan Corbin he would later add to his CI Playbook, an excerpt of which is below:

Jack Turner's CI Playbook
The Essential Elements of Competitive Intelligence: The Extended Elevator Speech

- First and foremost, competitive intelligence is a legal and ethical activity. We're not breaking into the Sanders estate to steal the colonel's secret recipe for tasty chicken. We're not sending spies to work at Google to decipher the top-ranking factors in its algorithm. We're not hacking into any computers. We're not breaking into any locked filing cabinets. We *do not* engage in espionage, spying, or any type of cloak-and-dagger activities.

- It's important to create a clear CI strategy. What is the purpose of the CI unit? It is designed to enable growth, mitigate risks, inform short-term or long-term plans, address strategic or tactical needs, or a combination of all six of these elements. It is also important to determine the governance around CI. If there are competing needs or priorities, who will make the determination on where to focus CI's finite resources?

- Conducting secondary research, also called open-source or desk research, is table-stakes as part of a CI function these days. It's a great foundation on which to build but that alone provides no unique advantage, because everyone has access to that same information. How this information is interpreted and used in combination with other insights is what matters.

- Where allowed, we *do* reverse-engineer products to fully analyze and understand construction and composition. We *do* engage in rigorous primary and secondary research. We are not the CIA or MI6; rather, we're more like investigative journalists or coaches for professional sports teams scouting the competition.

- How do we obtain private information using straightforward legal and ethical methods? Think of an hourglass. The sand at the top is a company's private information. As that company conducts business across the global supply chain, its private information eventually trickles down into the public realm just as the sand trickles down to the bottom of the hourglass. In the end, a good chunk of private—*not* secret—information becomes public information, and to the rest we apply analysis to figure out the answers and gain perspective.

- Primary research in CI is all about finding and talking to the right people with knowledge on the topics you're researching to gain perspective. You may ask, why would an employee of a competitor's supplier, for example, share any of the information we seek, especially when we truly identify who we are and for whom we work? When you do the hard work and find the right people to speak with, you *will* find people who know things and are often willing to talk. Part of it is human nature to share what you know, to correct you when you're wrong, to teach and coach—it's all part of the approach. It comes down to getting enough pieces of the puzzle to see the picture. You don't have to capture secret information to figure out what a company is doing. Sometimes you can handle this work in-house, but for other situations you may need to get outside help with the research and analysis.

- Classic elicitation techniques are fundamental to the conversational aspects of CI work. Some techniques that John Nolan makes reference to in his book, *Confidential,* which include naivete, bracketing techniques, *quid pro quos*, flattery, quotation of reported facts, feigned disbelief, and word-repetition, and are all important tools in the CI toolbox.

■ This is one of the key elements that separates CI from traditional market research and data analysis. CI involves people *actively investigating* the competition—suppliers, customers, regulatory issues, basically any external forces that could affect the business plan—by *talking with other people*. Because traditional market research relies more on viewpoints of the present, or on publicly disseminated information that's available to everyone, or on the use of more traditional survey instruments and questionnaires, it is mostly rooted in the past and present. CI is unique because it provides a glimpse into the future by actively gathering the information that is not always published, and converting that information into insights through analysis that provides impact on a company's strategy and/or tactical decisions. And just because certain information isn't "published" doesn't mean it isn't publicly available; one just has to ask for it.

■ We also keep detailed records about where the information we gathered comes from. This practice not only protects us from charges of illegal or unethical conduct, but it also helps us build a network of reliable contacts and sources, and eventually, a database that can be tapped into and relied upon.

■ When primary and secondary research is complete, we process, analyze, and write up our findings, because in the end, CI is about providing a unique perspective. Real, actionable intelligence can be a godsend in the planning and decision-making process.

■ CI professionals are not in the "nice-to-know" business. We focus our often-limited resources on areas stakeholders "need to know" and figure out those answers as we verify and validate various inputs and produce outputs that help drive strategy at the corporate, regional, product, or functional level—much like a hub-and-spoke framework.

4

THE OFFER

JACK'S CHEST SWELLED as he looked across the luxury box to see Sofia and Keri laugh and cheer, their faces illuminated by the enormous scoreboard hanging in the middle of the United Center. His daughter, now sixteen, had seemingly morphed from tadpole to full-grown overnight. Jack sighed, knowing he would blink and tomorrow Keri would be flying the coop for college, joining her older brother, Cody.

"You have a beautiful family," Ryan Corbin observed, handing Jack a drink.

"Thank you," Jack answered. "And thank you for inviting them. What a nice surprise. You're just full of them today."

Shortly after their lunch meeting, Corbin had called Jack, asked to keep the conversation going at the Bulls game that night—wife, kids, and all. There was even a sleek black Cadillac Escalade sent to pick them all up. It got even better when Jack and his family were escorted up to the swanky luxury box Corbin's investment firm owned.

"Thank you for coming at such short notice," Corbin said. "I appreciate the fact I put you on the spot today. I wanted to make it up to you."

"Not at all," Jack replied. "All you really did was ask about what I do for a living. I believe in CI and I have a passion for it, so it was a bit of a softball question."

Corbin laughed freely and easily looking even younger than his thirty-six years—his age was one of the first things Jack had Googled after their lunch.

"I'm glad you see it that way. And now I hope you don't mind if I really do put you on the spot." The smile was gone and now Corbin's youthful face turned serious. "It's my understanding that intelligence is, in part, used to make sure companies aren't caught off guard. No surprises. With an in-house CI function, how is it possible that Hewitt never saw Apricus coming? As the head of that program, how is it that *you* never saw it coming, Jack?"

Jack felt the full weight of the past month's events come crashing back on his shoulders. After a moment, he shook his head. "I blew it."

As if on a cruel cue, the crowd cheered. Corbin let Jack collect his thoughts. "I knew, my entire department knew, that the threat of a new competitor was high. There's just too much money, too much growth in gaming. We also knew that a smart potential competitor would suss out and we were always on the lookout for new market entrants, but with a narrow focus. In-house, we referred to it candidly as our 'blind spot.' Addressing that blind spot required a significant investment. To look beyond our direct competitors and expand our scope to the entire market as a whole, we needed additional people and resources. I tried to get that investment, but I failed. So, long story short, Apricus caught us by surprise for a simple reason: they were in our blind spot. And I didn't push hard enough and acted assertively enough to get senior leadership to understand and believe me."

Corbin nodded. "First, I appreciate you taking accountability. That's real leadership! From where I'm standing, you did your job, detected a threat, brought it to the C-suite. Horse to water, as the old saying goes." He rubbed his chin, musing, "Hypothetically: what if you had been successful in getting the buy-in you wanted back then? What would your department look like today? What would you have done differently?"

"Not just my department, the entire organization," Jack said without hesitation. "When I say additional people and resources, I mean I wanted to integrate CI *across* Hewitt Games, embed it into the culture."

Corbin raised his brow. "Not sure I understand."

"A CI-supportive culture," Jack said, unable to hide his enthusiasm. "You're familiar with the behind-the-scenes, labor-intensive work we do digging out shreds of information from external sources. Well, imagine if CI was embraced within Hewitt Games, top to bottom, and everyone was encouraged to provide knowledge, insight, data, perspectives, tips—you name it. I'm talking about leveraging Hewitt's greatest strength, its talented people, to create an internal, human-sourced intelligence network to complement and enhance our existing external networks."

Ryan nodded. "Intriguing."

Jack sighed and shrugged. "Of course, in order for that type of cross-functional collaboration to become a reality, you have to break down the walls, transform the culture. And for competitive intelligence, no less?"

"But I thought CI was embraced at Hewitt? After what happened during the last console refresh, the dust-up with Sampson after Howard Hewitt passed."

"Formally a part of Hewitt Games, yes," Jack answered, shaking his head. "But fully embraced? We still have separate market-research and data-analysis teams, and getting them to share information with my CI folks can be like pulling teeth. The old adage 'information is power' is still at play here." Jack stopped himself. "Please, understand, this is not me trying to throw anyone under the bus. I would never—"

"Jack, I get it. Department heads with their own teams and budgets, their own voices they want to be heard, the professional egos. No need to explain. I'm just trying to get a clear picture, a better understanding. Please, continue."

Jack looked at his wife and daughter again, saw Keri wave, and waved back. "As you probably know, there is still a great deal of misunderstanding when it comes to competitive intelligence. Is it market research? Is it data analysis? How is it any different from business intelligence?"

Corbin put up his hands, feigning fear. "Keep that corporate espionage away from my company!"

Jack smiled. "Believe it or not, I actually ran out of my first meeting with Bob Laurence when he told me he led Hewitt's CI program. Literally ran out of the restaurant!"

Corbin threw his head back and laughed.

"It's a jump for any company to formally add a CI program," Jack continued. "To integrate CI throughout the organization fully, to create a CI-supportive culture where competitive intelligence is aligned with the various stages of the strategic-planning process? We're talking about a Neil Armstrong—level giant leap. Susan Wright made the jump, she just wasn't quite ready to moonwalk, and I fully understand why."

The arena buzzer sounded, signaling the close of the quarter. Sofia and Keri rose and joined Jack and Corbin. They talked about basketball, Keri's schoolwork, and their life-altering experiences with the Covid pandemic. When the girls finally excused themselves to hit the Madhouse Team Store pro shop, Jack and Corbin moved to two of the box's first row seats overlooking the arena. They watched as a team of cheerleaders led by Benny the Bull launched t-shirts into the stands with three-person slingshots.

"So do you think we can pull it off?" Corbin asked.

"Beat Apricus? I'll admit, I do have my doubts," Jack confided. "But I'm feeling much more optimistic after speaking with you at lunch."

"Getting back on track and beating Apricus is the goal," Corbin insisted, "but do you think we could achieve that goal by integrating CI throughout Hewitt Games, creating this CI-supportive culture you describe to gain insights that inform our investment decisions?"

Jack nearly spit out his drink. "Taking on a transformation like that is a challenge at the best of times. Now, during the war with Apricus we suddenly find ourselves in?"

"Indulge me," Corbin said. "A thought exercise. Walk me through how we'd go about it."

Jack shook his head, but his mind raced as he considered the possibilities. "We'd have to start at the very top with company leadership or there's no chance. Board and C-suite CI champions."

"I just so happen to have an in with the board," Corbin said with a smile. "Beyond top-level CI champions, what next?"

"Educating our people on what CI is and isn't," Jack said. "Take competitive intelligence out of the shadows, show everyone there is nothing to be afraid of. And we need all to contribute at some level."

"That extended elevator speech you gave today, some form of that would be a good first step," Corbin nodded.

"Follow that up with internal marketing and branding of the CI unit," Jack said, picking up the rhythm. "Connecting our real, talented people, their names and faces, to this mysterious function."

"The people *and* their work," Corbin added. "Profiles of the CI unit's campaigns."

"Agreed. We'd couple that with regular recognition of all staff members who contribute, encouragement for everyone to take part. Of course, we'd need sophisticated two-way information-sharing technology."

"And don't forget the cherry on top," Corbin said. "The results. Regularly sharing our CI successes, the positive impact, the return on investment."

Jack laughed. "Not ROI, but ROCI—Return On Competitive Intelligence, as we say on my team. Well, it was actually a metric I picked up from a group called Proactive Worldwide. It's a new, slightly different metric than traditional ROI or just Return on Assets or Return on Equity … ROCI focuses specifically on the value of Competitive Intelligence."

"That's terrific," Corbin enthused.

Jack snapped his fingers. "Congratulations, Ryan; we just developed the roadmap to creating a CI-supportive culture in"—Jack counted on his fingers—"six steps."

Jack noticed Corbin was suddenly flashing his pointy white canines. "I suppose the next piece would be an interim CEO to champion the CI transition."

"Interested in pulling double duty?" Jack asked with his own grin. "Chairman of the board and interim CEO?"

"Me? No, I'll have my hands full with the board. You'd be surprised. What about you?"

If Jack had any liquid left in his mouth, this time it would have ended up all over the patrons below.

"I'm serious," Corbin insisted. "Who better to create a CI-supportive culture, bring all of Hewitt Games' intelligence together under one voice to help us formulate our future moves and countermoves based on intelligence, not anecdotal information or gut instinct?"

Jack couldn't speak, move.

"What do you say, Jack?" Corbin pressed, throwing his arm over Jack's shoulder. "Want to lead a transformation that business school professors will be teaching their students about in twenty years?"

Later that night, a stunned Sofia would ask Jack what his reply to Ryan Corbin had been. Jack answered honestly: "I don't know. I think I blacked out."

Jack Turner's CI Playbook
Steps to Creating A CI-Supportive Culture

Steps to Creating a CI-Supportive Culture

1	2	3	4	5	6
Have at least one C-suite champion	Educate people regularly on what CI is and isn't	Brand and internally market the research unit	Know and profile the research function's clients	Encourage and recognize staff contributions	Regularly share successes/impact

1. Have at least one C-suite champion

2. Educate people regularly on what CI is and isn't

3. Brand and internally market the research unit

4. Know and profile the research function's clients

5. Encourage and recognize staff contributions

6. Regularly share successes/impact

5

EXPECTATIONS

"*S*OLVITUR AMBULANDO," SOFIA said, kissing Jack on the cheek as he headed for the front door.

Jack truly believed in the Latin phrase, loosely translated as "it is solved by walking," and frequently put it into practice. Whenever he had a particularly vexing issue he needed to noodle over, he would lace up his sneakers and call out, "*Solvitur ambulando!*" as he threw open the door. This time Sofia beat him to the punch.

The partly cloudy weather matched Jack's disposition. Similar business stories had played out enough times throughout the years to have become cliché: an activist investor bulldozes into an organization with big plans to right the ship, but with no real experience in the industry, and only succeeds in quickening the ship's descent to darkness. Was Ryan Corbin the square peg to Hewitt's round hole?

Down the steps of his modest townhome in the heart of Old Town, Jack turned east, destination Lincoln Park. He hoped the greenery would lighten his mood. The linden trees and monuments passed in a blur as Jack, as if on autopilot, set course due south. Through the Gold Coast and Streeterville he trekked as the sun continued to jockey with the clouds for position, his own thoughts shifting from positive to negative and back again. West along the River Esplanade, Jack hit the massive Merchandise Mart before he stopped among the bustle of pedestrians and recognized where his subconscious was taking him.

He quickened his pace up North Wells into the River North neighborhood, feeling the warmth of the sun on his face as it finally broke through the clouds. Past the art galleries and restaurants, Jack arrived at his destination: the former home of the Chicago Fire Department's Engine Company 42, the one-hundred-and-fifty-year-old, three-story, brick-and-mortar building Bob Laurence now affectionately called HQ.

Jack rang the buzzer and waved into the security camera, hoping the old man was still pulling six-day workweeks and would be in the office on a Saturday. Sure enough, the door flew open a moment later.

"Forgot I lost my 'No Solicitations' sign," Laurence said with a smile. "Must have thrown it at the last salesman who came knocking."

"What if, and this is still entirely undecided, it was the new interim CEO of Hewitt Games who came knocking?"

Laurence crossed his arms over his barrel chest, looked Jack up and down. "Now *that* is a gentleman I would consider inviting into my place of business."

After describing in great detail the events of the previous evening with Ryan Corbin, Jack collapsed into a leather armchair in Laurence's conference room. The walk from home to the old firehouse was under two miles in total, but mentally Jack felt like he'd run a marathon.

"Just like that," Laurence enthused with a snap of his fingers, "knowing you for less than a day, speaking with you for, what, an hour total, he offers to make you chief executive of the world's biggest console-gaming company?"

"Technically, interim CEO," Jack replied, sinking farther into the armchair.

"And he not only wants you to completely transform the company culture with CI, he wants you to do it while the stock is near all-time lows and the wolves are at the door?"

"If by wolves at the door you mean fending off financial ruin at the hands of a global e-commerce juggernaut in the form of Apricus, then yes. The wolves are at the door."

Laurence exhaled a deep breath and sunk down next to Jack in a matching armchair. They both remained there, slumped and silent, as an antique wall clock ticked away the minutes.

Jack broke their silence. "Corbin is dealing himself quite the hand here, isn't he? Kept coming back to that thought the whole way here."

"A hand that could make him look like the savior of Hewitt Games—or just as easily, make you the scapegoat for the downfall," Laurence replied.

"Susan Wright warned me he was a shark, that he was always two steps ahead."

"Two? From where I'm sitting, that kid is already waiting at the finish line."

"What would you do?" Jack asked.

"You know me, glutton for punishment. I'd take the job, make the CI-integration we've talked about for years a reality, use the full might of Hewitt Games to figure out how to shoulder-check Apricus back into its e-commerce lane."

"And Corbin?"

"The team you've built over the past ten years is top-notch, people you can trust. You won't be alone, no matter what Corbin is up to." Laurence looked over, offering a smile. "But this isn't about me. What will *you* do, Jack?"

On the walk home, the sunset framing Chicago's skyline in violet and orange, Jack called Andy Barrows. His old friend gave Jack the laugh he needed and a line of encouragement that made Jack's heart swell: "I've known you since we were dorky teenagers in college. I've seen you grow into an amazing husband and father, and a tireless, respected leader. I'm honored to call you a friend and colleague, and I can't imagine a better man for the job. Jack, you were made for this."

Sofia sat waiting on the stoop, reading a book under the entryway light, her blond curls glowing. She smiled when she saw Jack coming, folded a page corner and closed the book in her lap.

"So tell me, was it solved by walking?" she asked.

Jack pulled his wife up and wrapped his arms around her. "We're a team. I can't solve anything without your help, no matter how many miles I walk."

"CEO positions don't just fall from trees," Sofia reminded him. "Even interim ones. Though, admittedly, this one certainly dropped into your lap."

They both laughed before Sofia continued. "It won't be easy, but this is an opportunity you can't pass up."

Jack let his cheek rest on top of her curls. "I was hoping you would say that."

After dinner, sitting down in his home office, Jack took a deep breath and made the call to Ryan Corbin. After a minute of small talk, Jack dove in.

"In CI, we're required to manage expectations on just about every project thrown our way," Jack said. "Part of it is due to the myths and misunderstandings around CI that we've talked about. Part of it is due to corporate culture, which tends to be reactive instead of proactive. Part of it—"

"I think I know what you're getting at," Corbin chuckled. "Don't worry, Jack. I know you don't have a magic wand. I know CI, even if we can successfully integrate it throughout Hewitt, isn't a silver bullet that will solve all of our problems."

"That's a relief," Jack answered. "And it's my hope, as a former CEO of a wildly successful company, you'll help this very new chief executive learn the ropes and be a true collaborator from your position on the board. Regular, open communication."

"Absolutely, Jack. Whatever happens, we're on this grand adventure together."

"I'm going to hold you to that," Jack said, meaning it.

"As well you should. And please remember, collaboration is a two-way street."

"Understood," Jack replied, taking another deep breath.

"So, are you saying what I think you're saying?"

"If you think I'm saying, 'I'm in,' then yes, you are correct."

Corbin laughed.

"Let me try that again," Jack announced, clearing his throat. "Ryan, I'm in."

6

REFLECTIONS

JACK'S ENTIRE HOME-OFFICE resembled an evidence board from a detective drama, with charts, reports, pictures, and handwritten notes pinned and taped to all four walls.

"This isn't something you see every Sunday morning," Sofia said with wide eyes, nudging into the file-filled office with two mugs of steaming coffee. "Since when did you start moonlighting as Sherlock Holmes?"

Jack laughed and eagerly accepted the caffeine. "More like Inspector Clouseau, only much smarter."

Sofia sat down cross-legged on the floor, her back to an armchair loaded with boxes of files. "All right inspector, fill me in before I call Andy Barrows and tell him he needs to come over to check on you."

"Right," Jack began, placing his mug down on the only clear corner of his desk. He gestured around the room. "All of this represents my last ten years at Hewitt Games, most of the work and projects I've led as Chief Competitive Officer. This is how I built Hewitt's CI function."

"So, a timeline of sorts?" Sofia asked, rubbing the sleep from her eyes.

"No, it's not chronological; at least it's not meant to be. It's putting all of the data, all of the history in front of my eyes so I can see all of the obstacles—pinpoint the hurdles and issues we faced along the way. Nice refresher course, to boot. Here, let me show you."

Jack walked to the far wall. "This is a big project we worked on way back in 2013. Susan Wright and her folks wanted insight on releasing a smaller form-factor console. Essentially all of the same parts and components but designed and implemented in a way that would create a smaller package. As an aside, one of the biggest complaints we hear about gaming consoles is that they are big and ugly, and people don't like the eyesores in their living rooms."

"They certainly aren't pretty," Sofia nodded.

"Agreed," Jack said. "This case is a great example, because my team stumbled headlong into a number of hurdles that we would repeatedly see again and again, project after project, over the ensuing years."

"Example?" Sofia asked.

Jack unpinned a report with multiple bar charts. "Time," he said. "Leadership felt that the tactical, transactional work we were doing was consuming too much time. They wanted quick answers, but they failed to fully grasp the volume of work my team had to do, the time we had to invest in order to provide actionable intelligence. Now, if the CI function had been fully involved in the strategy and planning process, that would have been another story."

After shuffling to the side, Jack had another report in his hand. "Here. This issue goes hand-in-hand with the work consuming too much time: Deliverables are not timely to enable decisions on business priorities and strategies. When a CI function is reactive instead of proactive, it loses potency. In order for CI to be most effective, it must become aligned with the various phases of the strategic-planning process."

"And this big number two," Sofia asked, pointing to the Post-it note on the report. "I'm seeing it all around the room, along with some other numbers. You're finding the issues and labeling them?"

"Precisely!" Jack beamed. "By looking at all of the work collectively, I've been able to pinpoint the obstacles we've consistently faced, the impediments to making our CI program a highly-valued function."

"I'm seeing a lot of tens," Sofia noted.

Jack pulled another report and tapped the Post-it with the number ten circled. "Resource constraints," he nodded. "Whether it's budget, talent, technology tool—we bump up against old number ten here all the time."

Sofia stood and began a museum walk around the office. "I'm beginning to see the method to your madness. By identifying the issues you've commonly faced in establishing the CI program at Hewitt, you're preparing yourself to face these obstacles again when you essentially start from scratch and work to establish a CI culture across the entire organization."

"If I had a badge, I'd name you an honorary deputy," Jack said. "The good news is, we aren't starting from scratch." Jack picked up his open laptop, unplugged the power cable, and stood beside his wife.

"Bob Laurence has been helping companies implement CI functions for years. He has the insight and data to know what works and what doesn't. He's been sending me everything he has, and it's been a huge help." Jack found the file he was looking for and clicked on it. "Here we are. This chart outlines how CI functions advance in an organization. I'd say we're already at the intermediate or established level in a number of categories but have a way to go to have the impact we really should."

Evolution Of CI Functions*
Although some activities can be accelerated, building a successful, world-class operation typically takes ~5 years

Start-up: 1–2 years	Established: 3–4 years	World-class: 5+ years
Assign a strong CI champion	Develop it as an integral tool	Embed CI in the culture
Complete a needs assessment	Deliver project-based CI	Engage in dialogue-based CI
Identify core stakeholders	Establish product/service lines	Integrate tactical & strategic CI
Complete ad hoc demonstration projects	Apply a CI blueprint/analytical framework	Deploy advanced CI analytical tools
Create function strategy and structure	Develop vendor relationships into partnership	Participate directly on key business leadership teams
Conduct CI awareness training	Coordinate all CI activities throughout the company	Contribute significantly to bottom line results
Develop delivery/CI platform	Formalize the CI evaluation process (ROI)	Become a trusted CI partner
Build an internal/external network	Focus on outcomes	Offer BU-specific CI solutions
Institute a kit process to prioritize focus	Reduce uncertainties	Demonstrate thought leadership
Identify key CI vendors/partners	Engage in scenario planning	Develop an agile CI capability
Develop a CI code of ethics	Establish an early warning system	
Engage in war gaming workshops		

* Based on the authors' combined 60+ years of experience working with leading organizations. Portions Adapted from Herring-Leavitt 2011 World-Class Competitive Intelligence Program Roadmap.

Sofia looked over the chart. "I see assigning a strong CI champion at the top. Fairly certain I know a new CEO that will take the lead to rapidly evolve the CI function to add more value in no time."

Jack kissed his wife. "That he will."

Jack Turner's CI Playbook
Top Ten Hurdles / Impediments To Building A Highly Effective Intelligence Capability

1. Deliverables lack actionable business insight and recommendations

2. Tactical / transactional work consumes too much time

3. Intel team talent lacks business or market understanding and/ or critical analytical skills

4. The corporate function ignores BU / Regional issues

5. Deliverables are not timely to enable decisions on business priorities and strategies

6. Information is delivered or data is dumped, and the analysis burden is left to the recipient

7. There are inconsistencies in local capabilities and the ability to execute against needs

8. Competing priorities inhibit any real, valued outcomes: BU, Regional, and Local

9. Routine reporting lacks insight (newsletters tend to diminish the CI function brand value)

10. Resource constraints: CI leadership, talent, budget, meeting / process integration, and technology tools

PART TWO

The CI-Driven CEO

7

ONE VOICE

HEWITT GAMES APPOINTS JACK TURNER INTERIM CEO

CHICAGO, Ill. /WireNews/—Hewitt Games Corporation (NYSE: HWTG) (the "Company") today announced that its Board of Directors has appointed Jack Turner, the Chief Competitive Officer of Hewitt, as Interim Chief Executive Officer, effective immediately. This appointment follows Susan Wright's decision to step down as Chairman and CEO of Hewitt. Board member Ryan Corbin was named Non-Executive Chairman and will lead Hewitt's search for a permanent CEO.

"This is a critical time for the Company, and we are thankful Jack has agreed to take on this challenge," said Mr. Corbin. "With more than a decade of experience leading Hewitt's CI function, we are certain Jack has the knowledge and experience to become a strong interim CEO."

Mr. Corbin continued, "We're especially excited by Jack's unique skill-set and great appreciation for the external environment as we work to transform Hewitt into an organization

*that delights its customers and provides value for its share-
holders. Some CEOs have sales backgrounds and the company
becomes driven by a sales focus. Others come from marketing,
operations, or engineering, and their respective areas of expertise play a huge role in how they run the company. With Jack's
background in CI, we're confident and hopeful Hewitt will
become an intelligence-driven enterprise that always makes
the best possible decisions for its customers and shareholders
based on intelligence, not gut or anecdotal information."*

JACK MADE THE choice on the morning he walked into his old office
on the forty-second floor of Hewitt Games for the first time as
interim CEO: the CEO's corner office would remain vacant until
Hewitt officially named Susan Wright's successor.

If, and it was a *huge if*, Jack managed to succeed in this grand
endeavor—create a truly embedded, CI-friendly culture at Hewitt
and beat Apricus, shed the interim title, and become chief executive—then he would officially move. If not? Well, as Jack had joked
with Andy Barrows, he would in all likelihood be emptying out his
old office anyway, so why risk two moves?

Andy Barrows, sitting across from Jack, laughed at the joke, but
quickly turned serious. "I can't imagine a better first decision. Show the
troops that you're humble, that you plan to earn everything you get."

Jack shrugged. "I suppose. It would also take a few days for me to
move and get fully settled, and those are days we simply don't have
to waste. That and the fact that I hate moving."

"Ugh, who doesn't?" Barrows laughed as he rose from his seat.
"But I'll make you this promise before I go: *when* you officially make
the move to Susan Wright's old office, I'll be here with a stack of
boxes, ready to help you lug everything down the hall."

"Those banker's boxes, with the built-in handles and secure-fitting
lids?"

"Of course! What do you take me for, some sort of cardboard-box
philistine?"

"And they come flat but pre-folded so they pop together with ease." A voice came from the hall. "No tape required. Truly the pinnacle of box technology."

Andy turned and stepped out of the way to reveal Julie Sawyer, Jack's trusted right hand from the CI team.

"Now, there is a woman who knows her cardboard," Andy said with a laugh.

Julie had been at Jack's side from the very beginning, working the first legendary CI project that saved Hewitt from being blindsided by Sampson Electronics a decade ago.

"Julie," Jack greeted her, checking his watch. "Right on time, as usual. Andy, if you'll excuse us, we can pick up the cardboard box discussion later."

Julie sat as Andy departed and looked around the office. "All this talk of boxes, but it looks like you're staying put?"

"I am," Jack said. "No time to waste. Which is why I'll get straight to it: Julie, your work ethic and knowledge of this company's CI function are unmatched. I would be honored if you would step into the recently vacated position and become Hewitt's new Chief Competitive Officer."

Her eyes widened. "But with you becoming interim CEO, I just assumed you would be pulling double duty. Have a fallback in case, you know, things go south? Oof, sorry, it's not that I think things will go south—"

"It's okay, Julie. I never would have taken this role if I wasn't fully aware of the circumstances. The bottom line is, in order for this to work, I can't just dip my toes in and pull them back out if the water is too cold. I have to dive in. And I wouldn't be diving in if I wasn't 100 percent certain I'm putting the CI function in good hands. You've earned this promotion and you deserve it."

Julie beamed. "I … I don't know what to say, Jack."

Jack stood and extended his hand. "Say you'll accept."

Julie stood and gave a firm shake. "I accept. Thank you so much for the opportunity. I won't let you down!"

"I know you won't." Jack sat back down. "We'll talk about your new compensation later. Now that that's settled ..."

~

"Now more than ever—in a post-Covid business world filled with so much uncertainty—it's critical that we bring all of our intelligence together under one umbrella. Data Analytics, Market Research, Consumer Insights, Competitive Intelligence: we need to be able to use these various, often disparate channels as the lynchpin of strategic collaboration throughout this entire organization, from the first floor all the way up to the forty-second."

Jack paused for dramatic effect and to quench his thirst. He went around the conference table, as he took a drink of water, looked all of the department heads and board members in the eye, saw Ryan Corbin give a slight nod.

"We can achieve that goal by making competitive intelligence the one voice within the company that brings all traditional intelligence together. One voice that channels all of the amazing data, the primary and secondary research, customer or user experience, and analysis our teams do. One voice that serves as the magnetic needle in Hewitt's compass, always pointing true north."

Jack caught the first sign of displeasure from the corner of his eye: COO Fei Hong rubbed her temples. In a similar manner, across the table, Chief Financial Officer Amar Patel began stroking his beard. Jack wasn't sure, but it also looked like Amar gave a slight shake of his head in disagreement. They were both subtle about it, but the message was clear: the pushback had begun.

"I get it," Jack continued. "There is still a great deal of misunderstanding about CI, what it is, and how it's done. One of my first priorities will be to clearly define this new intelligence function for all stakeholders and ensure any misunderstandings are cleared up as quickly as possible. The important takeaway here is this: the goal is to build a powerful, unified intelligence capability that is embedded in all aspects of our strategy and planning. Why is that critical to Hewitt's success going forward? Because our intelligence function won't simply pump out more data. It will offer objective judgments, insights, perspectives, and analysis to enable us to make better decisions.

Certainly, CI alone isn't going to turn this situation around. It also takes our sales, marketing, innovation, and other groups, along with our brand loyalty to reclaim our dominance. But CI will play a major role to support and drive our decisions."

Jack picked up a copy of the *Wall Street Journal* and began to walk around the conference table. "Brick by brick, we *will* create this intelligence capability, and we *will* align it with our business objectives. We *will* leverage the strengths of the talented teams within this historic company that Howard Hewitt built. And we *will* explore the unknown as we determine how to respond to Apricus in the most effective way possible, and take action to prevent us from being blindsided again."

Jack paused to read a headline and raised an eyebrow. "It's interesting, these daily articles from financial experts and analysts predicting our impending doom: they never once mention the more than one-hundred million subscribers to our Primo Live service. That's one-hundred million active, loyal Hewitt customers worldwide—a group that has more than doubled from the forty million we had back in 2016, and that, by all metrics, loves our products and service."

Jack tossed the newspaper onto the conference table. "Wall Street seems to think that this fight is over, that Apricus has already won. Reading these headlines, it's almost as if they are seeking our surrender. My response to Apricus, the financial media, and our one-hundred million loyal Hewitt fans everywhere is simple: as John Paul Jones expressed it, we have not yet begun to fight."

Jack Turner's CI Playbook
Best Practice Strategies For Effective Implementation

- Define the function's purpose for stakeholders
- Align CI-outputs with business objectives/strategies
- Be an informed, trusted partner
- Produce high-quality deliverables
- Cultivate an independent, objective viewpoint
- Watch for bias
- Be clear on what services you offer and what you don't

8

IMPACT

OVER THE YEARS, Jack had bent Amar Patel's ear on a fairly regular basis, hoping the CFO would become a powerful ally in the push to support and expand the CI function. Those calls were ultimately fruitless, as Patel would always patiently listen to Jack's pitch before responding bluntly, "Show me the ROI."

While Susan Wright believed early on, she never truly championed CI as fully as necessary and hadn't been the kind of believer Howard Hewitt had been. That's why, on a nearly-annual basis, Jack would find himself repeating the frustrating loop: seeking support from the CFO so he could better document the real and substantial return on investment from CI—the ROCI. Then got pushback from Patel who first wanted to see the hard-number ROI before he would consider jumping on board. A catch twenty-two worthy of Joseph Heller himself.

Jack understood that what Amar truly needed was a push from a C-suite CI champion, a believer at the very top of Hewitt Games that Jack had never had. Until now.

Jack knocked on Amar's half-open office door and saw the CFO look up from his laptop with a resigned expression.

"I was wondering when you might come calling," Amar said. "Thought you would summon me to your spectacular new office. Then I heard that you didn't actually move."

"Word travels fast around here," Jack said. "Staying put. For now. And I'm shooting for a management-by-walking style. Good excuse for me to get my steps in." Jack laughed, gesturing to the chair that faced Amar's desk. "Is now a good time?"

Amar offered a polite smile. "How can I help?"

Jack sat and crossed a leg over his knee. "I was thinking about a line our friend and former colleague Bob Laurence is fond of: talk is cheap, but it takes money to buy whiskey."

"Whiskey?"

"A placeholder, I suppose. Knowing Bob Laurence, there's a lengthy tale attached about whiskey and dauntless men from the early 1900s. Regardless of what is being bought, the point holds: it's easier to say you'll do something than to actually do it."

Amar leaned back. "We have not yet begun to fight …"

Jack laughed. "Touché. So let's talk whiskey, or rather, results, specifically in the form of return on investment, ROI."

"I believe R-O-C-I was always your preferred acronym?"

"So you remember." Jack grinned. "And here I thought my pleas about a return on competitive intelligence went unheard."

Amar took a deep breath. "Heard, yes. Seen? The bottom line is that I have difficulty seeing the true monetary value competitive intelligence provides. The anecdotal results are certainly impressive, and I'm not arguing that there aren't benefits, but I deal strictly in numbers garnered from facts and data. I need the valid data, Jack."

"Terrific," Jack replied without skipping a beat. "So let's determine how to calculate the return on competitive intelligence. What do you consider to be valid data?"

"I'm sorry?" Amar stammered.

"There are multiple formulas we can apply to determine ROI for CI. I want to make sure the CFO of the company has direct input in selecting a reasonable, defendable model Hewitt values and believes in."

"I see," Amar said, sitting forward in his seat, forming prayer hands as he began to think. "I'm familiar with your function's work, of course, but I'll certainly need additional information and specific details about the scope of projects, time, resources."

"Our new Chief Competitive Officer, Julie Sawyer, is already working to put a package together for you," Jack answered. "For now, let me tell you what I told Ryan Corbin when he asked for the competitive intelligence extended elevator speech."

Patient, as always, Amar listened attentively as Jack went through the core of the function: legal and ethical practices, how actively investigating differentiates CI from traditional research tools, and how analysis of primary and secondary research data produces actionable intelligence.

Amar seemed most interested in the detailed records Jack and his team kept on each project, asking a handful of questions about the CI database and how work was charted: personnel time, salary and labor cost, training, conferences, travel, equipment, and so on.

"I know it's a lot to chew on, but based on this preliminary information, what are your initial thoughts on a formula for determining the ROI of CI?"

"Well, I know qualitative measures bear weight, for example, how CI stimulates discussion, generates new ideas to solve problems, things of that nature. But it's the quantitative measures we've got to nail down. You mentioned Primo's online subscriber base at the meeting today. Quantitatively, we can look at our customer-retention numbers or things like Net Promoter Score (NPS) to determine customer-satisfaction improvement. These metrics will naturally have an impact on revenue and profitability …."

"Great place to start. I'm sure you agree that estimates in some qualitative measures are required. There are real benefits there, and we're shooting for perspective more than precision."

"Certainly. As I said, they bear weight."

"Excellent," Jack said, standing to leave. "I'm confident we'll work together to prove the true value of intelligence to Hewitt Games.

We're already off to a fast start. Julie will get you all the CI information you could ever possibly need. Then we need to make defining the specific metrics we'll measure to determine ROCI a top priority. We'll need that data to prove we're not just talking about the power of a CI transformation at Hewitt; we're actually doing it and producing real results."

"Buying whiskey, yes," Amar replied, still in deep thought. "Oh, and Jack?" he said, catching Jack at the door. "I hope you know what you're getting into here. I have my doubts about what the true numbers will show, this ROCI you so ardently believe in."

Jack grinned as he departed. "That, Mr. Patel, is why you're the perfect man for the job."

Jack Turner's CI Playbook
Key Principles To Consider
When Calculating Roci

- Often, according to Kenneth Silber in his 2002 publication, *Calculating Return on Investment*, what the stakeholders consider to be valid data *is* the valid data—obtain direct input from key stakeholders.

- Strive to work closely with the CFO/financial analyst and create what pharmaceutical industry intelligence expert Neal Mahoney refers to as conservative, reasonable, believable, and defendable assumptions to help prove the value of intelligence for the company.

- Primary areas that should be measured based on feedback from users of intelligence and industry expert Jan Herring: time savings, cost savings, cost avoidance, revenue increase, and value added.

- Other areas include client retention, customer satisfaction, employee retention, market share, productivity improvements, profits, quality, reduced reaction time, and surprise avoidance.

- Estimates are okay if they are acceptable to stakeholders; strive for perspective over precision in determining qualitative benefits.

Key CI Function Metrics

SEVERAL POTENTIAL AREAS EXIST TO SHOW VALUE

QUANTITATIVE MEASURES

- Increased win rates
- Cost savings
- Cost avoidance
- Faster decisions / slower reaction time
- Improved market share
- NPS / Customer satisfaction improvement
- Customer retention

- Increased revenue
- Increased profitability
- Time savings
- Enhanced customer experience
- Increased number of intel users
- Extension of product life cycle

QUALITATIVE MEASURES

- Stimulation of new thinking and discussion to solve problems
- Avoidance of surprises
- Leadership learns something new
- CI drives/supports M&A actions
- Boost in leadership confidence in making the right investment decisions

- More effective strategies
- Contributions to the business plan
- Ideas for new products / services
- Leadership goes to CI to understand meaning of market shifts
- Positive testimonials from leadership

9

INTELLIGENCE FRAMEWORK

ACREW FROM BUILDING services, in their forest-green jumpsuits and hauling tables, chairs, and equipment down the hall, drew a crowd. Executives up and down the forty-second floor leaned out of office doorways to see what all the commotion was about.

Jack turned the corner and nearly ran into a man carrying a filing cabinet. He looked around the human train of office goods and saw they were all headed to the end of the hall on the right. The corner office. The office that Susan Wright had left behind and Jack had decided to leave vacant.

Sidestepping workers and equipment, Jack made it to the end of the hall and squeezed through the door. In the middle of the room, framed by the floor-to-ceiling windows and the breathtaking view of Chicago's skyline, Ryan Corbin stood, directing traffic.

"Ryan, what's all this?" Jack asked over the clamor.

"Jack, hi!" Corbin replied, flashing his pearly whites. "Heard you weren't taking this incredible space, figured why let it go to waste?"

Jack nodded as he made his way to Ryan's side, crossed his arms and then uncrossed them, trying to avoid being confrontational. "Quite the collection of furniture you're bringing in!"

Ryan laughed, slapping Jack on the back. "It's not for me. Well, maybe a chair. Welcome to the CI war room!"

"Ooh," Jack murmured, relieved but fairly certain he was the unwitting victim of a Ryan Corbin power-play.

"Swung by your office earlier to give you the heads-up, must have missed you."

"Right, I was on a bit of a management walkabout, checked in with some folks. Most notably Amar Patel."

Now Corbin crossed his arms. Jack noticed. "Our intrepid CFO did not appear pleased when you announced our CI one-voice initiative."

"That he did not. But his skepticism comes from the right place, and it actually makes him the perfect man for the job. Determining the monetary benefits, the true value of CI in regard to impacting the bottom line, has always been a challenge. Having a skeptic create the ROI formula would be scary *if* I wasn't 100 percent certain of the immense value CI provides. When it comes directly from the CFO of Hewitt, it will be undeniable. Amar Patel is going to be the intelligence function's best friend."

"Look at you," Ryan observed, uncrossing his arms. "First official day on the job and you're already forging critical alliances."

"No time to waste," Jack said, stepping around office chairs. "Let me know when we're set up. I'll get to work putting our transformation team together so we can get this war room buzzing."

Jack checked his watch when he strode into the newly-christened CI war room, stunned to see the now lit-up Chicago skyline. "Almost seven already? I have to call my wife."

"Welcome to CEO life, where the entire world seems to run on fast forward," Ryan Corbin said. He gestured around the room. "What do you think?"

Jack looked up from typing a "Sorry, running late" text to Sofia and was stunned again. Susan Wright's former office looked unrecognizable. Long wood conference tables, digital whiteboards, and fully-equipped workstations with cameras for video calls made the room look like one of the hip new shared-office spaces popping up all over the Chicago Loop. Jack looked back out the door and down the hall to make sure he was in the right place.

"Wow."

"Just the response I was shooting for," Ryan said.

Jack walked around the space, taking it all in. Impressed and excited to work together with his team in this room, he also couldn't help but wonder if this would ever actually become *his* office. Had Ryan just subconsciously revealed his hand—a set of cards that only ever had Jack as the temporary CEO? Jack shook the thought away and placed the laptop he held under his arm on a table near a set of ports.

"These whiteboards up and running?" Jack asked, plugging in.

"IT gave the thumbs-up, but you'll be the first to put that to the test," Ryan said, walking to Jack's side. "What have you got?"

"I was going to send this to you, but right now feels like the perfect inaugural use of the war room."

A few settings clicks, and the digital whiteboard mirrored Jack's laptop screen. "We have lift off," he said, sorting through digital files before he found what he was searching for.

"'Intelligence Transformation Framework,'" Ryan said, reading the graphical slide's title out loud.

"Exactly," Jack answered. "We've talked about the importance of educating everyone on what CI is and isn't, clearly defining the function. I realized today in speaking with a number of team leaders that we also have to clearly define how this intelligence function we're creating will be integrated with our business. Hence this framework."

Intelligence Transformation Framework

Effective intelligence functions have a clear purpose, governance structure, and well-defined capabilities that integrate with leadership meetings where decisions are being made. There is no "one size fits all" model.

STRATEGY & STRUCTURE	CAPABILITY
Strategy	**People**
What is the purpose of the CI Function?	Dedicated or Partial CI Staff?
Drive Growth? Mitigate Risks?	Talent / Skills / Experience Required?
Strategic? Tactical?	Type of Source Networks (internal, external)?
Support Long-Term Initiatives? Short-term?	
	Process
	Understand Needs
	Scope Project Requirements
	Collect / Store / Access
	Legal & Ethical Guidelines
	Analyze / Synthesize
Structure /Governance	Alerts, Reports, and Presentations
Where does the CI function reside?	Decisions and Feedback
Who determines the CI priorities?	
What leadership partnerships must exist?	**Technology**
Where and when do key decision-making meetings occur?	Reporting and Distribution Portals
How does CI best integrate with these meetings?	CI Platforms to Automate Collection of Secondary Research
	Social Media Monitoring Software
	Analysis Tools
	Visualization Applications
	Project Management Programs
	Storage - Central Repository Tools

"I'm noticing a lot of items in the Technology block," Corbin noted. "More than I would have thought."

Jack nodded. "One of the reasons I wanted to put this up on the big screen for you. We knew that using technology to encourage two-way sharing of intelligence would be a critical piece to the puzzle. Putting together this framework made me realize how essential it is, and how much work we need to do to get there. Technology and things like CI platforms will help enable the intelligence capability, but they are not what creates the intelligence. We still need the human minds for that!"

"I assumed your CI department already had something in place, something we can build on?"

Jack sighed. "Budgets being what they are, technology is an area I was never able to advance for the CI function. We're firmly rooted in email and have occasionally tapped Hewitt's intranet. Sure, we have access to some subscription tools but not the kind of central repository that we need."

"A CI web portal?" Ryan asked.

"Nothing close. We've got to get from beginner to advanced in a hurry, with sophisticated information-sharing tools that will make the CI web portal we never had look lame."

Ryan clapped his hands and rubbed them together. "We're heating up now, aren't we?"

Jack laughed. "I expected this news to dampen your enthusiasm."

"I love a good challenge," Ryan enthused. "And it may be a smaller portion of your slide compared to technology but look at Structure and Governance."

Jack smiled, understanding where Ryan was headed.

"*Intelligence leadership and partnership in key business areas,*'" Ryan read aloud, patting Jack on the back as he read the slide. "Check, check! '*And intelligence integration into key business processes and meetings.*' Check and check!"

"I have to admit," Jack said, "as the guy who struggled for a decade to bring CI into key Hewitt processes, to find even the hint of a partnership with top leadership—it's a good position to be in."

"It's a *terrific* position to be in," Ryan agreed as he closed Jack's laptop. "Now go home to your family and get a good night's sleep. Tomorrow, the real work begins."

10

INTELLIGENCE INTEGRATION

J ACK WOKE BEFORE his alarm and started his morning jog before the sun rose. He showered, dressed, and departed before his family began to stir, and pulled into Hewitt's underground parking garage before the night security staff gave way to their day counter-parts. *I think I like this,* he thought; *living in the Before.*

As Jack turned toward the parking spot reserved for Hewitt's CEO, the one Howard Hewitt himself made sure he arrived at first daily so that every other employee entering the building would see his car, he found he wasn't the only one fond of the Before.

A few spots down, the parking garage's lights gleamed off of a sleek black sedan. Save for James Bond movies, Jack had never seen anything quite like the car's amalgamation of vintage and new, exotic and refined.

Sure enough, up on the forty-second floor, hunched over his laptop in the new CI war room, sat Hewitt's own mysterious special agent, Ryan Corbin.

"Didn't expect to see anyone this early," Jack greeted Ryan, looking at his watch and thinking, *At least he didn't take my parking spot.*

Ryan looked at his own watch and stretched his arms out wide. "Actually, it's late for me," he said, stifling a yawn. "Too late. Afraid I fell deep down into the Portal forums rabbit hole."

Portal, the online platform for Hewitt's Primo console, was, for all intents and purposes, Hewitt's current product. The Primo Platinum console, now roughly eight years into its life cycle, had reached a market saturation point roughly three years before. Then came a wave of virtual reality-hardware add-ons and accompanying games, spurring sales and extending the traditional five-to-six-year life-cycle of the console.

Now that the VR wave had subsided, Primo sold only a smattering of new units each month. That made Portal, with its paid subscriber base, digital game sales, streaming video channels, and advertising, the lifeblood of Hewitt until the next Primo launched and the cycle began anew. Of course, that typically smooth new console generation-transition was now very much in doubt thanks to Apricus and Sovereign, the cloud-gaming platform aiming to obliterate traditional gaming console hardware altogether.

"I've been down that rabbit hole myself a few times," Jack said, sitting down across from Ryan. "But before I ask you what you learned, please, for the love of all things holy, get up out of that chair, go home, and get some sleep."

Ryan checked his watch again, shook his head, closed his laptop, and began gathering his things. "You're right. I can still catch a few hours; get back here before our kick-off meeting."

"One question before you go," Jack added. "Will that amazing car I saw in the garage lift off the ground and fly you home on autopilot?"

Ryan laughed as he hit the door. "For what I paid for it, it should."

The CI war room buzzed. If Ryan Corbin had done nothing else for Hewitt during this turnaround and decided to resign from his board position and walk away from the company today, he still would have scored a home run. Creating this war room, locating it in this amazing space, and outfitting it like a dream collaborative workspace had been a brilliant idea.

The proof was in the pudding. The cross-functional transformation team, this Center of Excellence or Advisor Council Jack had gathered for their first meeting gushed like a group of teenagers at a concert before the curtain goes up. And then the star walked in. Showing no signs of wear from the all-nighter he'd pulled, Ryan Corbin—dressed casually in a black t-shirt and chinos—waved and smiled sheepishly, joined Jack at the head of the main conference table. The chatter calmed briefly, then rose to a crescendo.

"Like it or not, you make an entrance," Jack said.

"No, no," Ryan replied, unpacking his laptop. "It's this room. Someone once said if you love the space where you work, you'll love the work that you do."

"If that holds true, based on everyone's response thus far, Apricus is in trouble," Jack declared, raising his arms for attention. "All right, everyone, if you could find a seat and get comfortable, it's time we got this kick-off meeting started."

Jack took stock of the team as the members took their seats: Ryan representing the board of directors, CFO Amar Patel, Chief Marketing Officer Amanda Givens, COO Fei Hong, new Chief Competitive Officer Julie Sawyer, and Chief Technology Officer Brad Whitman. Jack knew he had allies in Ryan and Julie Sawyer, believed he was heading that way with Amar Patel, but knew there was still much work to be done with the CMO, COO, and CTO. That work was about to begin.

After a brief introduction, Jack began his presentation with the extended CI elevator speech, continuing his ongoing effort to clearly define and educate Hewitt about the function.

"Some of you have heard this speech already, others of you more than once. But it's critical for us to continually educate everyone on what CI is and isn't."

He shifted to Hewitt's existing CI function, where it was, and how it needed to advance in the organization to become the "one voice." He shared the intelligence-transformation framework he'd created to better define how this one voice would be integrated into Hewitt Games, highlighting the need for the rapid deployment of a two-way intelligence-sharing network.

"Julie, you and Brad will run point on this," Jack said. "We'll discuss this in greater detail soon, but as you can see in this framework, the efficiency we create with this sharing network will be the bedrock that we build this transformation on."

Jack capped off the presentation with a slide illustrating the ultimate goal: integrating intelligence with the planning process.

"This is where the rubber will meet the road," Jack continued. "When we achieve this goal, Hewitt's strategy and planning processes will be tied directly to the intelligence function, and vice versa. This is where the one voice we're establishing will have the greatest impact."

"Transformations of culture and processes within an organization are challenging at the best of times," Jack continued. "As you are all well aware, these are far from the best of times at Hewitt Games. With Sovereign, Apricus is actively working to send traditional consoles the way of the Dodo bird. That is why we must pursue this intelligence-function transformation as we actively work to determine how best to respond to Apricus and Sovereign."

"Isn't there a particularly unflattering adage about fighting a war on two fronts?"

The question came from COO Fei Hong, and sitting next to her, CMO Amanda Givens nodded in agreement. Jack recognized he would likely be facing pushback not just from individuals, but also potentially from an alliance.

"These are distinct challenges, to be sure, but we undoubtedly face a single front with Apricus," Jack replied. "Though, you used a fitting description, Fei. That's because I believe we can make great strides toward creating a CI-supportive culture and determining how to best respond to Apricus in one fell swoop. Hewitt is going to war, in this case via a business war game."

Ultimate Goal - Intelligence Integrates with Planning Process

Strategic & Annual Planning Processes	Q1	Q2	Q3	Q4
Corporate Strategic Plan	Research & Preparation	Scenario Workshop / Refinement	Strategic Plan development / communication	Board Presentations
Division Annual Plans	BU planning / reporting	Research & Preparation	Strategic Plan development / communication	
Current Business Performance	Quarterly Bus. Review	Quarterly Bus. Review	Quarterly Bus. Review	Quarterly Bus. Review
Pressure Testing Competitive Strategies	Facilitate Business War Game	Facilitate Scenario Planning Workshop		Facilitate Indicators Workshop
Competitive and market Intelligence	Market Entry Assessment	New Competitor Profile		Competitor Function Profile
Customer Insights	Customized Comparative Journey Map			Customized Customer Usability Study
Competitive Monitoring and Alerts	Timely and relevant insight on market movements, competitors, and conferences			
Training and Coaching	On-going intelligence function development and training			

Illustrative

Effective CI units align their outputs with various phases of the strategic planning process to optimize impact and value

"War game?" Amanda asked, glancing at Fei. "Given the current cir-cumstances, is that really how we want to invest time and resources?"

"The circumstances make it the perfect time," Ryan interjected. Jack was relieved to remember he wasn't alone. "A business war game is something we can orchestrate and enact fairly quickly and at a relatively low cost in terms of time and money. So a minimal invest-ment with a potentially transformative outcome, both in terms of our transition as a company and how we respond to Apricus."

"I see," Amanda responded, still not sounding convinced.

"This won't be just any war game, mind you," Jack emphasized. "This will be Hewitt's own unique brand of CI war game, where the intelligence we gather on Apricus and Sovereign will be critical in how the exercise plays out.

"I, we, appreciate the questions and concerns," he continued. "Part of this process, and this CI war game in particular, will be to foster cross-functional collaboration and teamwork. In other words, we want to hear your voice."

"Thank you," Amanda replied. "I've never been one to keep quiet."

"That's a good thing," Jack said. "Keeping quiet is the last thing we'll need for this CI business war game to work."

Jack Turner's CI Playbook
The Benefits Of War Gaming

Business war gaming invites companies to challenge stifling, siloed internal practices, encourages collaboration, and fosters cross-functional teamwork. The communication and creativity war gaming fosters results in an enterprise-wide increase in driven, cohesive strategies. Benefits include:

- Align leadership on the market and competitive landscape

- Develop thinking for strategic moves and countermoves that increase your probability of success when market and competitive uncertainties become reality

- Enable better decisions by clarifying and prioritizing strategies and raising awareness of possible competitive actions

- Redefine business plans and investment priorities and set market and competitive intelligence monitoring requirements

- Foster greater internal collaboration and bring down silos

11

SILENT TREATMENT

THE WINDY CITY lived up to its name as Jack hustled up North Rush. He popped his sport coat's collar against the biting cold and blew into his clasped hands as the wind pulled bright leaves from the maple trees lining the block. It felt good to get out of the office, even if it was only for a quick lunch, but as each leaf flew by, Jack felt time slipping away.

Apricus had, thus far, only revealed Sovereign. No firm release-date beyond "next year" had been announced, and no one outside of Apricus had gone hands-on with the streaming gaming service. Not yet at least.

Internally, Jack's team worked with a best guess that Apricus would open Sovereign with a series of beta tests, probably beginning in the early spring and continuing through the summer, before a formal launch of the product in late fall. Just in time for the holiday season roughly one year from now.

Hard facts flattened that seemingly ample cushion: Hewitt had already planned on a reveal of its new Primo console at the annual Electronics Entertainment Expo, E3 for short, in June, followed by a November launch—roughly one year from now. Years of work and hordes of treasure spent on market research, designs and concepts, software, marketing campaigns, components, and the corresponding supply-chain partnerships were now suddenly thrown out the window.

If the company were to continue on schedule and launch its Primo against a new technology designed to make traditional consoles obsolete, Hewitt could be staring down the barrel of a historic flop not seen since Coke decided to change up its secret recipe with New Coke. Jack recalled New Coke had lasted all of three months before Coca-Cola clumsily reintroduced its old formula as Coca-Cola Classic. The proposition made Jack swallow hard. If Hewitt released its own New Primo clunker, in all likelihood there wouldn't be a Primo Classic to fall back on.

Jack turned into Gibson's restaurant and sat across from Bob Laurence, thankful to feel the warmth inside the old steakhouse and ready to shift his thoughts away from Primo, at least momentarily.

"What have you got?" Jack asked.

The older man shook his head. "We've talked about Ryan Corbin being two steps ahead, but I'd say he's closer to a chess grandmaster who has plotted out checkmate in about six moves."

Jack planned to lean heavily on Laurence's experience and expertise in the coming months to help him determine Hewitt's best strategy. He also had a secret side project for his old friend: to shed light on what Ryan Corbin was really up to.

Laurence pulled a folder from his briefcase and opened it on the table. "This Schedule 13D filing flew under everyone's radar about three years ago. A small investment firm out of Florida by the name of Amet Ventures opened a sizable stake in Hewitt Games."

"Amet Ventures? Doesn't ring a bell," Jack said. "How sizable of a stake?"

"Almost 13 percent. And I'll give you a hint about Amet Ventures: *amet* in Latin translates to English as 'fun.'"

Jack shook his head. "Fun ... as in Ryan's online toy retailer Funporium? Are you sure Amet isn't a surname or something? You must know who runs it."

"I do know. But only after digging. See, Amet Ventures is owned by another company, that's owned by another company, and on down the line. All legitimate, mind you, but it's clear the principals wanted to distance themselves from Amet Ventures's moves, and keep their names out of it. And yes, you are correct. Fun as in Funporium, as in the company that Ryan Corbin sold for billions."

The server came by to take their drink order. On reflex, Jack said, "Coke Classic." When the waitress departed, he lowered his voice and leaned forward confidentially. "So, you're saying Ryan actually started buying into Hewitt Games three years ago?"

Laurence nodded. "He did. Not only that, but Amet Ventures sent this email to Hewitt's then-CEO and Chairman of the Board, Susan Wright. This unknown investment firm, with a suddenly sizable stake, questioned why Hewitt was delaying the launch of the next console generation. They recommended the board scrap plans to extend the current console lifecycle with virtual reality add-ons."

Jack took the printed email and quickly skimmed its contents. "'Time is not on Hewitt's side,'" he read aloud. "'At best, Hewitt will have one more extended traditional console cycle before the technology for streaming gaming services advances to the point where consoles like Primo are no longer required.'" Jack dropped the letter.

Laurence enunciated, "Grand. Master."

"So, Ryan saw this coming three years ago, bought in so he could make his voice heard by Hewitt's board, and issued a warning that no one heeded. His prediction comes true—"

"And suddenly Susan Wright is out, and Ryan has a seat on the board," Laurence finished.

"Talk about activist investor," Jack said. His Coke arrived and he took a swig. "So, this is all positive news, isn't it? Now we know this isn't just something a bored billionaire did on a whim. He's been following Hewitt and the market in great detail for years. He truly wants this to work, and he doesn't have a secret plan to strip the company and sell it for parts."

"That's my read on it," Laurence concurred.

Jack drank again, absentmindedly wondering what New Coke tasted like. "One piece that doesn't quite fit, though: why did Ryan double down on his investment? He already had a sizable stake, likely would have gotten his board seat once he revealed he was behind Amet Ventures. Why pour in additional millions when the company is in the very same worst-case scenario that he'd predicted?"

Laurence tapped his forehead. "Grandmaster stuff, that. With his latest buy-in, he lowered his cost basis per share by roughly half from when he originally bought at Hewitt's peak. Simultaneously, he single-handedly stopped the company's stock slide, convincing analysts, brokerages, and whale investors everywhere that wunderkind Ryan Corbin *must* know something that they don't. All that, and now he gets to *really* throw his weight around, make truly bold moves. Proved as much when he tapped you to take over."

"I suppose. And with me as his handpicked interim CEO, he can throw around his weight not just with the board, but the entire C-suite, as well."

Laurence laughed. "And let's not forget, he's put himself in a position to get all the credit if you succeed or pin all the blame on you if things go south."

"Grandmaster is right," Jack said, slumping back in his seat. "I suppose there's only one thing for me to do."

Laurence smirked. "And that is?"

"Make sure things don't go south."

Jack felt the knot of stress in his shoulders loosen ever so slightly after his meeting with Bob Laurence. Still, knowing he served as Ryan Corbin's veritable canary in a coal mine was unsettling. He feared his next meeting would do little to lift his spirits.

"Is now a good time?" Amanda Givens asked with a light rap on Jack's office door.

"Amanda, yes, please come in. Grab a seat."

They exchanged small talk about family, Covid experiences, and the rapidly turning Chicago weather. The opening chat concluded with a laugh and a comfortable silence before Jack broke things open.

"This is, admittedly, crazy," he said.

Amanda gave a slight chuckle and furrowed her brow.

"Me, the competitive intelligence guy, suddenly CEO of the biggest console-gaming company in the world. On top of that, I'm leaning into CI, a function that's a mystery to most. I'm pushing to make this capability the core of a Hewitt culture change, and I'm doing it while the clock is ticking on developing a strategy to counter Apricus. Apricus, only the biggest e-commerce company in the world, flush with cash, and in possession of a cloud-gaming technology advancement that could very well make our consoles little more than huge, unsightly paperweights. Like I said, crazy."

As Jack spoke, Amanda's eyes grew wider and wider. When he finished, she sat silent for a moment before a chuckle escaped her lips and led to an avalanche of laughter. Jack joined her.

"I have to admit, I was afraid you were oblivious to the optics," she laughed, wiping away a tear. "I appreciate your being frank with me, Jack."

"A wise person once said, 'It is what it is.' And the fact is, we simply don't have time for corporate ego. I will always be open and honest with you, Amanda. All that I ask is that you do the same with me. That said, I know a single conversation does not make a professional relationship."

"That's true," Amanda replied, sitting forward. "I also know you wouldn't be having this candid conversation with me without a reason. What's the reason, Jack?"

Now it was Jack's turn to slide up in his seat. "I'm going to be asking a great deal from everyone at this company over the next few months. It's you though, who I'll likely be asking the most of." Jack paused to collect his thoughts. "As Hewitt's chief marketing officer, you are the company's chief storyteller. You create the narrative about our brand and invite our customers to take part in that tale.

At the same time, you're a protector of our brand, adeptly choosing what, when, and how we share news and information."

"Candor and flattery. Now I know you're going to ask me to do something I don't necessarily want to do."

"I'd say it's something no other executive at this company has ever asked you to do: *don't* share our story. Not until we're ready. Now more than ever, we need you to protect our brand."

"I'm sorry?" Amanda asked.

"Our ongoing marketing campaigns for games and Portal promotions, of course, full steam ahead. What I'm talking about is the story of this transformation. My story, Ryan's story, the story of how we're planning to counter Apricus. The story that countless news outlets have been asking you for *ad nauseum* for the past week. For now, the very most I want you to give anyone who asks is something along the lines of, 'We won't talk a big game, reveal our cards to the competition, we'll let our actions speak for us.' And feel free to fall back on the tried and true, 'No comment.'"

Amanda put both hands up, sat up taller, and took a deep breath as her face flushed. "Marketing exists for good reason: we shape the narrative. In this case, we have an opportunity to reshape the narrative that happens to be making us look bad. Very bad. And our story is really quite simple: how the beloved, historic console-gaming company will fight back against the big, bad e-commerce villain under the guidance of one of the most successful young entrepreneurs in history and his hand-picked choice of chief executive."

"That is absolutely part of the story we'll tell," Jack rejoined. "When we're ready. We're just not there yet."

"Staying silent allows the competition, the press and the pundits to speak for us, say we're not sharing our plan because *we don't have a plan.*"

"Sake of argument, we do a media blitz your way. Push Ryan out in front, make him out to be the golden boy savior of Hewitt. Inevitably, the core strategy questions will come. 'So, you've got Ryan; he's got his guy as chief executive, how do you plan to respond to Apricus?'

We'll say that we're working on something big, we'll share the details when it's time, and so forth. They'll push, ask again, wonder why a competitive intelligence guy was Ryan's pick? Ask, what the hell is competitive intelligence anyway? Then the journos and experts you trust will say the conversation will be off the record, maybe even offer a *quid pro quo* and provide information in return. So, you'll share more, knowing it's in confidence."

"I've been running Hewitt's marketing since you became CCO, Jack. I know who we can trust, the people I've established strong relationships within the press. I'll work very closely with Dawn Sanders, who I presume you know heads up our public relations team."

"The information you share wouldn't immediately make any headlines, sure," Jack said. "But I can guarantee you that the information you provide would make its way to Apricus."

"I disagree."

"I can guarantee it because I built Hewitt's CI program from the ground up, and a powerful tool in our CI arsenal is our network of journalists and industry experts. It's that same network that gave us the early warning about Sovereign, information we had before it was published for all to see."

"I see..." Amanda said, easing back into her seat as she put the pieces together.

"Just barely before it became public, mind you," Jack continued. "And that's a waving red flag that tells me Apricus has an adept CI function of its own and knew all the steps to take to ensure Sovereign was kept under wraps for as long as possible. Now let's say that the opposing CI function taps into their own network of journalists and gets the off-the-record information we shared. To hurt us, they can anonymously get that story out, paint the picture of how crazy this entire situation is, much like I did for you when we started this conversation."

"Crazy is right," Amanda mused, going quiet as she thought it through. She shook her head and stood, pacing back and forth behind her chair. Finally, she put both hands on the chair back with a resigned sigh. "Okay, Jack. Quiet it is. For now."

Jack expelled a deep breath. "Thank you. And I promise, there is an emphasis on *for now*."

"So what's next? If my team is muzzled, how can we help?"

"That's why I said you had one of the toughest jobs," Jack replied. "You won't be creating a narrative for the outside world just yet, but inside Hewitt Games? You're going to tell the story of the most amazing business turnaround in the past decade and you're going to invite everyone in this company to become a part of it!"

12

X'S AND O'S

JACK FOUND BOB Laurence's description of Ryan Corbin as a chess grandmaster fitting, and while he increasingly felt himself to be a novice in comparison, his opening gambit as chief executive at Hewitt Games began to take shape. Three weeks into his tenure, pieces moved across the board with determination.

Julie Sawyer, still getting used to her new title of CCO, juggled critical tasks with tenacity. Her compelling record of Hewitt's CI campaigns, a document that would serve as a potent educational resource for Hewitt's executives, was nearly complete. A companion document with even greater detail would serve as a rich data set for CFO Amar Patel as he worked to create the company's ROCI formula.

At the same time, Sawyer and her team worked tirelessly with CTO Brad Whitman to create Hewitt's sophisticated two-way information sharing tools, a feature-rich CI web portal which, even in its infant stages, made Jack wish he'd had the same technology years ago.

CMO Amanda Givens began to spin the transformation yarn for Hewitt's employees, while COO Fei Hong worked to establish the administrative and operating practices that would enable all Hewitt employees to contribute to the intelligence function. Despite Jack's best efforts, Fei continued to offer the most vocal pushback. He hoped she would see the light once Hewitt completed its first-ever CI war game.

The war game. Along with their other critical assignments, each member of the transformation team played a lead role in constructing the exercise.

Bob Laurence had run so many business war games for other companies over the years, he referred to himself as a war-gaming five-star general. As a consultant for Hewitt on the project, he led the transformation team's efforts as the war game facilitator, mapping out and designing clear objectives for the game.

If Laurence was the general, Ryan Corbin served as his lieutenant. The young entrepreneur worked such long hours with so little sleep, Jack began believing Ryan had been a mad genius Victorian-era inventor in a past life.

With Laurence at the helm and Ryan at his side, the CI war game rapidly took shape. The two-day event would take place at Hewitt's headquarters featuring four teams, each with five to eight cross-functional participants. The teams: Home team Hewitt Games, Competitor team Apricus, a Consumer and Market team, and a Control team comprised of Jack, Ryan, and Laurence running the simulation.

"Our keys to success, in getting the very most out of this war game, will be in our people and our CI-infused books," Laurence began, addressing the transition team in the CI war room for a war game planning session. "We've got to have the right people participating in their best roles. No pressure, Andy."

Laurence let out his trademark booming laugh and the team joined in. Jack had brought friend and colleague Andy Barrows on board to help plan and facilitate the war game because Andy knew Hewitt's staff inside and out thanks to his position as the head of human resources— hands-down the best choice to assign war game participants.

"I will recruit the best of the best, sir, general, sir," Barrows answered with a mock salute.

"At ease," Laurence boomed, drawing more laughs. "The second key will be our competitive intelligence-based books, as in the briefing books we write for participants on each team that will provide the knowledge, insights, facts, and perspectives they need to play their roles to the fullest. Facts based on the CI work we're doing to provide real, actionable intelligence. Amanda and Julie, what's our status on those books?"

"Still much work to do, but we're making good progress," Amanda replied. "We want to be sure they reflect the culture and character of the company participants will role-play."

As CMO, and a good one at that, Amanda Givens had the lay of the land in terms of consumers and competitors. She had all available secondary and published research on Apricus available, and her team was actively conducting polls and focus groups with consumers to learn more.

There was still a great deal of primary research about Sovereign that had yet to be unveiled, and that is where Julie and her team came in, with a CI campaign digging deep to learn everything there was to know about the cloud-gaming service. Thankfully, the work had begun immediately after Apricus's Sovereign unveiling, when Jack still led the CI function.

"We have our work cut out for us on the CI team," Julie cautioned. "But we have a few strong leads that we'll continue to develop."

Jack noted the two women were sitting together and genuinely seemed to enjoy each other's company. He knew that, if nothing else came out of this war game, marketing and CI were already forming a collaborative relationship.

"Just remember, briefing books are a balance," Laurence continued. "We want our participants to have the knowledge and insight about Apricus' strategy from a corporate standpoint, brand standpoint, marketing, sales, outlook, the whole package. But we also need participants to be able to absorb all of that data and insight in a short time frame, two hours at the very most. That means keeping the books to fewer than twenty pages. Keep the word 'briefing' top of mind."

Julie and Amanda nodded affirmatively.

"Along those lines," Jack jumped in, "remember that war-gaming is not about a detailed analysis where we dig down into the granular level of the environment. This is not a quantitative assessment. War-gaming is a qualitative, strategic level of interaction."

"Despite how Jack made that sound, I promise you, war games are not boring," Ryan said with a laugh. "This will be engaging and exciting."

"Thank you for correcting my executive-speak," Jack said. "Ryan is right, this will be fun."

"Fun and, if done right, war games *always* result in actionable outcomes," Laurence added.

"So let's nail it," Jack said. "How about our timeline? When does the fun begin?"

Laurence rubbed his chin. "Preparation for an event of this size is typically over two months, with half of that time spent on creating the briefing books. Considering our preliminary progress, the circumstances, and the talent of the team working on it, I think we can confidently get things rolling in half the typical time frame. This time next month is reasonable."

Jack opened the calendar on his laptop. "Let's say five weeks to allow us some wiggle room and to give us another week to get the most out of our CI-focused primary research projects. We're on the clock, but we need to get this right. No pressure, everyone, but we're likely to have only one shot at this. Let's not miss."

Jack Turner's CI Playbook
Planning A War Game

- A typical war game can take about eight weeks of preparation

- The first two weeks are spent planning the overall engagement and getting a clear understanding of objectives and logistics, determining who should participate, the exercises to run, and scenarios to play out

- Briefing book drafts can take up to five weeks to complete, maybe a little longer if additional primary research is required

- The final preparation week is spent adjusting briefing books where needed, finalizing event logistics, and placing participants in the right roles

- Plan for three or four teams—the Home team, one or two competitors, a Market team if required, and a Control team

- Teams should have five to eight participants, and each team should be cross-functional—best to put the company or brand leadership on the competitive teams, not the home team, so they can see their company from a different lens

- Plan on taking one to three days for the actual war game

- The Control team or facilitator for each team that runs the simulation exercise keeping the game on schedule, asking tough questions, and providing feedback to each of the teams

- War games use turn-based gameplay. At the start of each round, teams examine their current circumstances and make a plan before presenting their proposal to the entire group

- After first spending time to understand the competitive mindset of the key players, usually through a framework such as Four Corners, each team will role-play a particular "what if" scenario, and then present their moves and countermoves, then the entire group has the opportunity to challenge a team's outcomes, followed by the Control team opening and fostering a dialogue about the results

- In the ensuing rounds, teams attempt to counteract moves made in previous rounds or respond to any new shift or strategy that's injected

- If a Market team is used, it can award, for example, a certain market share to teams after each round based on who is "winning"

- Timelines are customized, with it spelled out at the beginning whether the discussion and debate are related to a particular timeline, say a month, quarter, or year

- War games produce real, prioritized actions; post-game leadership must define a clear set of responsibilities and assign taskforces to take the actions learned and make them a reality within an established time frame—in other words, determine what has to get done by when and by whom

13

NEW WRINKLES

KNOCKING ON DOORS.

The molten core of any CI campaign is robust primary research—a grind of dozens of calls and interviews to find small nuggets of useful information that are pieced together to eventually lead to insight and actionable intelligence. Though the process is done on a phone inside and behind a desk 90 percent of the time, Jack had long ago co-opted the phrase used by police to describe their own investigative grind.

"Let's get out there and knock on doors," Jack had told Julie Sawyer and the CI unit nearly a month before, officially unleashing the team on Apricus and Sovereign. Finally, weeks later, knocking on doors paid off.

Julie delivered the good news just before noon in the CI war room. "We've knocked on every door in town and then some, and I can say with a high degree of certainty that Sovereign will not launch with any exclusive new AAA games. We believe there are two independent studios working on small titles exclusively for Sovereign, but nothing that could significantly drive platform adoption."

Jack shook his head in disbelief. "We knew it was odd they didn't announce any exclusives at the Sovereign unveiling, but we assumed that would come next."

"That's not all," Julie continued. "Apricus is pushing for a seventy-thirty split on Sovereign, and, not surprisingly, as we discovered in some industry blogs, chat rooms, and posts on social media sites including Glassdoor, game publishers and independent developers are not happy. They might have trouble launching with a sizable library of old games, let alone new ones."

Jack knew the seventy/thirty split referred to the revenue model for digital game sales. Long the standard for digital marketplaces, it meant Sovereign would take 30 percent of any sale on its platform, while the remaining 70 percent went to the game's publisher.

"A revolutionary cloud-gaming platform, with an outdated, increasingly detested revenue model," Ryan Corbin noted, standing up from his seat. "And no massive launch exclusives? Ladies and gentlemen, we may have found the chink in Apricus's armor."

Hewitt Games itself used the seventy/thirty split for digital game sales on Portal, a huge source of the company's total income. However, Jack and his team knew pushback from publishers had recently risen to a fever pitch, with many game-makers describing the split as unjustified and threatening to pull their titles if the revenue model wasn't adjusted for the next console generation. Hewitt already planned on a shift to eighty-five/fifteen, possibly even eighty-eight/twelve.

"That is a swing and a miss of epic proportions," Jack crowed. "Sounds like Apricus is so focused on the technology of its cloud platform, it failed to grasp how critical its relationship with publishers and developers will be."

"I liken it to introducing yourself to someone for the first time, dressed to the nines, but with a joy buzzer hidden in your hand," Julie rejoined.

"Joy buzzer is the perfect description," Jack replied. "Let's get this data to Amar Patel and get a complete breakdown on launch games and the revenue model in our briefing books for the war game."

"Already on it," she answered.

"Great work, Julie! That's some valuable intelligence you captured!" Jack shouted after her as she hustled out the door.

Jack and Ryan faced one another as their thoughts percolated.

"If Apricus is using the outdated industry standard for its publisher-revenue split, what does that mean for its other critical revenue stream?" Ryan asked.

"Monthly subscriptions," Jack said with a nod. "Ten dollars a month for a streaming service is the standard."

Ryan nodded. "The revenue split is strong evidence they'll stick with the market standard on sub-pricing. The question now is, will they have enough games in their library at launch to justify that price?"

"Not just volume of games, but big, new triple-A titles. New movies and shows are what move streaming television subscriptions. Inevitably, it will be the same for Sovereign and games. Hell, it's what moves our consoles, always has been."

Ryan wagged his finger. "Like James Carville said in the nineties when he was running Clinton's presidential campaign."

Jack laughed. "'It's the economy, stupid'?"

"Exactly! Only in our case, it's the games, stupid. And the question is, will Sovereign have them?"

Fickle fate popped Jack's balloon of optimism that evening when his cell phone rang once, stopped, and was quickly followed by a second call. The Andy Barrows ring.

"Are you in front of a television?" Andy asked.

"One minute," Jack said, leaving his home office for the living room. "What channel and how bad is it?"

"Financial Network, *The Cliff Carlton Show*. Let's just say he's pushing all those stupid buzzers."

"That bad, eh?" Jack replied as he navigated to the program.

Carlton, a former hedge fund manager, served as the self-described voice of the retail investor, though his regular stock picks on his daily cable show suggested otherwise. Tonight, the animated host was even more blustery than usual, and the ticker below his red face made Jack's jaw clench.

HEWITT GAMES—TURNED UPSIDE DOWN

"This is a guy Ryan Corbin evidently pulled out of Hewitt's boiler room," Carlton barked. "Not only does he not have the experience or the skill set for this job, but he also clearly wasn't well suited to his previous position as chief competitive officer either, a.k.a., Hewitt's spook, little more than a corporate spy. This supposed watchdog allowed Apricus to strut into Hewitt's hen house without so much as a yip!"

Carlton hit a button on his cartoonish soundboard to trigger the sounds of chickens squawking.

"That, my friends, is the sound of your investment in Hewitt Games," Carlton went on. "And believe me when I say it's a rotten egg. My high-up sources on the inside tell me interim CEO Jack Turner fancies himself as some sort of turnaround guru, opting for a culture change at the once-great company instead of, you know, an actual plan to respond to Apricus!"

Carlton hit another button. Crickets chirped. "And that, my friends, is the sound of Hewitt Games throughout this entire fiasco. Jack Turner is telling loyal Hewitt investors nothing about his plans for the company. Why? Because there is nothing to say! He has no plans!"

More buttons slapped. This time producing bears roaring.

"To say I'm bearish on Hewitt Games is the understatement of the decade! Sell, sell, sell!"

Jack clicked off the television.

"Like I said," Andy offered after a moment of silence. "Lots of buzzers."

"We knew it was coming at some point," Jack sighed. "The hope was we would be able to get out in front of it after the war game."

"Sure, we planned on the 'No Plan' headlines, but what about

Carlton's 'sources on the inside' bit?" Andy asked. "Do you think we really have a leaker? Potentially even leakers plural?"

Jack's thoughts immediately went to Amanda Givens and Fei Hong. He believed he'd made great strides in building a relationship with Amanda, and he'd spoken with her directly about maintaining media silence. Did she finally decide to confide in one of her sources, knowing even off-the-record comments would make their way into the public discourse?

Fei Hong was the likelier candidate, with her continued and vocal questioning of Jack's strategy. But Carlton had specifically stated "sources." Given that it was all anonymous, the point was moot, but it did make Jack wonder.

Jack's phone buzzed with another call. Ryan Corbin's name showed on caller ID. "Thanks for the heads-up, Andy. Ryan is calling on the other line. Let's chat tomorrow, okay?"

"Sounds good," Andy replied. "Sorry to be the bearer of bad news!"

"I take it you saw *Carlton*?" Corbin asked when Jack flipped the call.

"I did. How that isn't considered a form of market manipulation, I have no idea," Jack said.

"Check the credits roll. A massive block of dense legalese all stating it's not investment advice, and the show is meant as entertainment only, yadda, yadda. Regardless, that won't make the outcome any less fun."

Jack laughed. "And what would that outcome be?"

"When we turn this ship around, crush Apricus, and force that button-pushing buffoon to give airtime to Hewitt Games' surging stock."

PART THREE

All In

14

A TIME FOR BUSINESS WAR

JACK TURNER HAD found sleep nearly impossible to come by in his first three months as interim CEO, and it had been an especially restless three weeks since Cliff Carlton had thrown him under the bus on national television. That made the morning of Hewitt's CI war game all the more startling.

The alarm clock stirred Jack from a deep slumber filled with pleasant dreams. The sun shone brightly through the blinds, and the song of the city rising played faintly outside.

Jack bolted upright.

Sophia's side of the bed lay empty. Jack looked at his alarm clock again and realized with audible relief he was waking up right when he was supposed to. Restless thoughts had been his internal alarm for so long, he'd forgotten he had a perfectly good clock set for a more than reasonable hour. Fully awake, Jack remained in bed to consider why, today of all days, he had slept through the night. He finally rose, confident in the answer.

The smell of fresh coffee directed Jack to the kitchen, where he found Sofia and Keri at the island, laughing over a tablet.

"What's so funny?" Jack asked, standing behind them to see what they were watching.

"The Internet," Keri said. "It's the gift that keeps on giving."

She lifted the tablet and pressed play for the video. Promptly, a toy poodle on its hind legs began frantically waving its front paws. Cuts to the dog in various scenes—in front of a houseplant, next to another dog, near a bed—all featured the same hind-leg-paw-waving dance.

Jack laughed. "Someone just off-camera is holding a nice big treat."

"Must be steak tartare to get the little guy so fired up," Sophia said. "Speaking of fired up, I can't believe you're still here. Isn't today the big war game?"

Jack squeezed his wife and daughter in his arms. "Couldn't leave without a good-luck hug from my two favorite girls."

"Mom's right," Keri added. "You've been out the door before sunrise for months. Did you get fired, Dad? Aren't you the boss? Did you fire yourself?"

Jack grinned. "No, I have not been fired, at least not yet. Yes, I have been up at ungodly hours and in the office before sunrise for months. And yes, today is the big war game."

"So what are you still doing in your pajamas?" Sophia asked.

Jack fetched a mug and poured himself a cup of coffee. "Well, I woke up with my alarm this morning for the first time in forever and wondered the same thing. Best sleep I've had in months. Finally figured it out: I've done absolutely everything within my power to prepare for this, and I know my team has, too. I'm ready. More importantly, I know Hewitt Games is ready."

~

Hewitt HQ hummed with activity. Jack arrived forty minutes before official business hours, and found the parking lot nearly full.

Inside, staff filled the building with animated conversations and smiles, and Jack spotted brightly-colored briefing books everywhere.

Though only twenty-six employees were taking part in the war game as official role-playing members of the Apricus, Hewitt, Market, and Control teams, Jack and his turnaround team had made every effort to involve the entire organization.

The week before, Hewitt officially introduced its fledgling Insights Hub, the CI portal developed by CTO Brad Whitman and CCO Julie Sawyer. The portal, designed to be a single point of access to information from internal and external sources, launched with robust content on the war game, including its goals, how it would be run, the teams, and each team's briefing books.

Jack knew the Insights Hub would be put to its first test today, as it would feature live-tracking of the war game. Hewitt employees were encouraged to log in and follow the progress of the game through the portal, take part with the ability to comment on each team's strategy, and serve as a sort of second Market team, voting to determine how to award market share to Hewitt or Apricus.

CMO Amanda Givens drove the successful early adoption of the Hub, creating a thrilling narrative around the war game, its stakes, and how everyone in the organization could participate in helping drive a cultural transformation at Hewitt Games.

With a hop in his step, Jack made it to the forty-second floor and found Andy Barrows waiting in his office.

"I've never seen this place so alive," Jack observed as he circled around his desk. "What do you thi— Andy? What is it?"

Jack saw the concerned expression on his friend's face and knew the morning's positive vibes were about to be turned down a few notches.

"I found the signed letter on my desk this morning," Andy said, sliding the paper forward. "Chief Operating Officer Fei Hong has resigned, effective immediately."

$\sim$

It wasn't how Jack envisioned starting the day with the turn-around team in the CI war room, but Fei Hong's abrupt departure had to be addressed.

"Cliff Carlton, claiming high-up inside sources, goes after Jack and the company, and a few weeks later Fei, the most vocal opponent of this transition, is gone without a word to anyone," Julie Sawyer said. "Too coincidental to be a coincidence."

"We can only control our controllables," Ryan Corbin said. "Let's focus on what her departure means for today's war game."

"She was on the Hewitt Home team," Bob Laurence stated. "We thought it would help create a Lincolnesque 'team of rivals,' with opposing voices and whatnot."

"We planned for potential absences," Andy reminded everyone. "Team member understudies, if you will. I've already spoken with Fei's second. She's eager to jump in."

"We'll be covered for the war game, but we need to look beyond today, as well," Jack said. "COO is a significant leadership role. Until we can find a strong replacement, we'll all have to chip in, absorb the responsibilities associated with the position."

"I'll dig into that," Andy replied, "and have a detailed breakdown of her responsibilities to you by the end of business."

"Good," Jack said. "Once that is in hand, we'll determine who is best suited for individual tasks." He stood and put both hands on the conference table. "I agree with Ryan in regard to controllables, but I also know that if I was running the CI function at Apricus, I'd put the full court press on speaking with Fei Hong. Recent history indicates she won't be shy about sharing."

"Jack is right," Laurence grumbled. "Apricus will likely have an in-depth look at our CI-focused transformation by the end of the week."

"I've already emailed legal about drafting an air-tight separation agreement," Ryan said. "At the very least we can make her think twice about what she tells anyone and risk violating her confidentiality agreement."

"The good news is she left today," Jack stated.

"Not sure I follow," Amanda Givens answered. "How was today of all days a good day for this?"

"Fei Hong knows everything about our CI transition, but she left before the war game started. She doesn't know how we're going to respond to Apricus, because we haven't determined that yet ourselves."

"Speaking of war games," Ryan said, rising while looking at his watch. "Places, everyone. The curtain rises in twenty minutes. Let's get this CI war game started and figure out what Fei Hong won't be able to tell Apricus."

15

FOUR CORNERS AND BLIND SPOTS

Hewitt's Insights Hub featured a countdown clock on the business war game page, and when it struck zero, CEO Jack Turner and Chairman of the Board Ryan Corbin appeared on a livestream from the CI war room.

"Good morning, Hewitt Games! Jack Turner here with Ryan Corbin and we're thrilled to kick off Hewitt Games' first-ever CI war game."

Jack heard a wave of cheers from the teams assembled in separate rooms on the forty-second floor. He even thought he could feel the enthusiasm reverberate up through the building.

"Wow," Ryan marveled. "Nice to know you are all just as excited as we are."

"Amazing," Jack joined in. "Thank you all so much for joining us and for taking part in what we believe will be a truly transformational event. We wanted to open with a few quick words and to make one point abundantly clear to the participants on our assembled teams and to all of you participating through the Insights Hub. That point is simple: speak up. We want to hear from you. The goal is real, cross-functional collaboration, and we can't have that unless everyone voices their ideas and opinions."

"If you are thinking something, say it," Ryan added. "If you're on a team, be incredibly candid and tell everyone what you really think. Don't hold back."

"The same goes for those of you commenting and voting through the Insights Hub," Jack continued. "We want your thoughts and objections. Give us the honest truth. Be real. This is not an affirmatory exercise to pat ourselves on the back. Also, let me remind you that all you see and hear during this event is confidential and should not in any form be shared outside of Hewitt. We don't want to lose our element of surprise."

"And understand that this level of open and honest collaboration can be uncomfortable at times among the teams, create tension, and even conflict. But conflict isn't necessarily a bad thing, if everyone remains professional," Ryan added.

"That's right," Jack said. "And don't worry, our war game facilitator, friend, and former colleague Bob Laurence will be there to monitor the temperature in the rooms, making sure conflicts and tension are properly directed to produce the best results. And speaking of best results, Ryan, why don't you tell everyone why we believe our war game could very well be the first of its kind?"

"Two words," Ryan replied. "Competitive intelligence. This isn't just a war game; it's a CI-infused war game or competitive readiness workshop. Thanks to the efforts of Hewitt's CI function, we've developed a great deal of insight into Apricus and its plans for Sovereign. This information has been incorporated into our briefing books to allow participants to not only think *about* the competition, but to actively take a role *as* the competition. To the best of our collective knowledge, this type of CI war game has never been attempted before at Hewitt."

"That's right," Jack jumped in. "And we'll use this invaluable data throughout our strategy workshops over the next two days. Most notably, in our Four Corners analysis. We've put a packet of information into the portal about it, but in short: it's a well-designed competitor-evaluation tool that will help us to further understand what Apricus plans to do from this point forward."

A chorus of boos filled the air. "That's the spirit." Ryan laughed. "But like my father always taught me, it's better to support what you love than waste time focusing on what you hate. So let's start this CI war game off right by supporting the company we love. Let's hear it for Hewitt Games!"

A louder cheer rose through the building as Jack concluded the kickoff with, "Let Hewitt's first CI war game begin!"

$$\sim$$

On Bob Laurence's recommendation, Jack had made the Four Corners analysis the cornerstone of the war game. The predictive tool, designed by business strategy legend Michael Porter, differentiated itself from other analytical models by pushing practitioners to understand a competitor's mindset and motivations.

What made Four Corners models in war games particularly effective, Laurence had told Jack as they prepared for the big event, was the fact that colleagues, role-playing as the competition, would give incredibly frank, accurate assessments of their own company.

"Know thy enemy *and* know thyself," Laurence grinned. "Sun Tzu himself would have loved a good Four Corners war game."

Coupled with the CI-infused briefing books that would allow participants to truly play as Apricus, Jack believed the war game would produce dramatic, tangible results.

Each team was given a clear set of goals for their Four Corners analysis:

1. Assess your competitor's mindset.

2. Use analysis to generate insights into the future.

3. Help identify the likely strategy changes your competitor might make and how successful they may be.

Jack and his Control team, with Laurence's guidance as project facilitator, would work to push each team's assessment forward with direct questions related to all four corners: Drivers, Current Strategy, Capabilities, and Management Assumptions.

As the game began and the teams started the war game off by digging into the briefing books and developing an understanding of the competitive mindset, Jack reviewed some of the critical questions the Control team would be asking, questions he would later add to his CI Playbook.

Four Corners Analysis

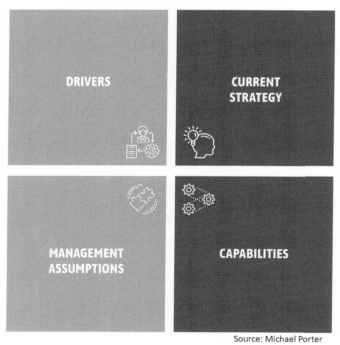

Source: Michael Porter

Four Corners Analysis – Described

MOTIVATIONS

Drivers

Analyzing competitor drivers and goals assists in understanding whether they are satisfied with their current performance and market position.

This helps predict how they might react to external forces and how likely it is that they will change strategy.

Management Assumptions

The perceptions and assumptions that a competitor has about itself, the industry, its customers, regulatory, other companies will influence its strategic decisions.

Analyzing these assumptions can help identify competitor biases and blind spots.

ACTIONS

Current Strategy

A company strategy identifies its unique positioning, how it will gain an advantage, and how it will sustain that advantage over time. How will the competitor compete in the market?

There can be a difference between the **"intended strategy"** (the strategy stated in annual reports or in public) and the **"realized strategy"** (the strategy the company is following in practice)

Capabilities

An organization's capabilities will determine its ability to execute its strategy and to initiate or respond to external forces.

When a strategy is producing satisfactory results, it is reasonable to assume an organization will keep competing in the same way.

Jack Turner's CI Playbook
Four Corners Analysis:
Key Questions To Populate The Four Corners

Motivation/Drivers:

- What goals are motivating competitor strategies?

- Where do they want to compete?

- What drives the competition to want to win?

- What business philosophy drives them?

- What elements of corporate culture motivate their plans?

- What are the unique traits of the leadership team?

- What external constraints drive their behavior?

Management Assumptions:

- What do competitors perceive as their strengths and weaknesses?

- What advantages do they believe they have?

- What do they assume about the market?

- What do they assume about current and future competition?

- What do they think about suppliers/buyers?

- What industry forces and trends influence their strategy?

- What do we know and believe about their plans and goals?

- What culture traits impact their strategy?

Current Strategy:

- What is the competition's current strategy? What is their unique positioning?

- How do they differentiate from others in the industry?
- Where are they investing?
- How do they drive new demand?
- How is their business creating value?
- What core relationships do they leverage that are part of their strategy?

Capabilities:

- What are the competition's core competencies?
- What gives them confidence they can execute their strategy?
- What is the key functional edge they can leverage?
- What leadership qualities exist to win?
- What is their financial strength?
- What IP do they possess that gives them an advantage?
- What skills do they possess that give them an advantage?
- What unique partnerships do they have?
- In particular, Jack wanted to ensure each team thoroughly addressed critical questions: What is your competitor's unique positioning? How are they going to gain an advantage? And how are they going to sustain that advantage over time?

While the Apricus and Hewitt teams targeted one another, the Market team was tasked with looking at both companies from the perspective of the consumer. To mix things up, the Market team, under the guidance of a Control team facilitator, would conduct a Blind Spot Analysis on Hewitt and Apricus from the lens of a customer to assess the positioning, assumptions, opportunities, and strategy gaps.

Blind Spot Analysis*

Company Leadership	Assessment
1. Satisfied with the company's overall current market position?	
2. Satisfied with customer perception of the brand?	
3. What are leadership's potential blind spots / gaps in its strategy?	
4. What key assumption is the company making that has to be true for its overall goals to succeed?	
Opportunities And Ability To Execute	**Assessment**
1. What specific market and product segment opportunities is the company targeting to realize its goals? What customer experience is it trying to create?	
2. What are the assumptions the company has about the overall opportunity (e.g., the size, scope, basis for differentiation, etc.)?	
3. What must the company be able to "do" with regards its goal in order to win?	
4. What are the risks / rewards? Where are its vulnerabilities?	

* **Source: Benjamin Gilad – Business Blindspots**
Typical blind spots: 1. Unchallenged assumptions 2. Corporate myths that motivate current processes/ behaviors 3. Emotion vs. fact-based strategies

After wrapping the Four Corners and Blind Spot analyses, the teams would then dive into a Strategic SWOT analysis in the afternoon, detailing the strengths, weaknesses, opportunities, and threats each company faced.

Round One would wrap up with each team sharing each other's findings, and Day One would then officially close with a preliminary market share vote by the Market team.

For months following Sovereign's unveiling, Hewitt Games had reeled under mainstream media bombardment and the subsequent dive in share value. This first vote, Jack knew, would serve as a far more accurate assessment of the situation than the current stock price.

Just how bad was it really for Hewitt Games? Jack and his team were about to find out.

16

FEEL THE HEAT

THE FIRST ANTICIPATED temperature rise came in the early afternoon. What surprised Jack is where it came from: the Market team.

"A combination of some participants relishing their roles while others are having trouble embracing them," Laurence said, leading Jack and Ryan down the hall. "This is the perfect time for the facilitator and the Control team to step in and direct the tension in a positive direction."

Jack felt the heat the moment they stepped into the room. On one side of the conference table, CFO Amar Patel stood with his arms crossed, shaking his head.

"'Open and honest' does not mean a green light for baseless attacks on the company you work for," Patel said, his head bobbing.

Carolyn Copley stood opposite Amar and served as his verbal sparring partner. As Hewitt's head community manager on Portal, Carolyn often served as the first point of contact for Hewitt customers to voice complaints. The console, the online platform, games, accessories—if something went wrong in the Hewitt-verse, customers often went directly to the online community forum Carolyn ran to post their grievances.

"These are not baseless attacks," she emphasized. "They are just a handful of the things I hear from our customers every single day. You want to know what the market thinks is a huge Hewitt weakness? It's that we don't listen to them, that we think we know better than they do."

Jack felt like he'd stepped into the room at the perfect time. And if Jack was being honest with himself, it also felt good to see Amar Patel standing up—literally—for Hewitt Games.

"Temperature check!" Bob Laurence called out as he swept into the room. "If you two wouldn't mind taking your seats, we can help direct this conversation."

Amar and Carolyn sat down, both looking slightly flushed.

"All right then, it appears this analysis has touched a nerve," Laurence noted. "Carolyn, why don't you expound on your point. You say a Hewitt weakness comes in the form of listening to its customers. Or rather, not listening to its customers. Can you provide an example of that?"

"The controllers," she replied without hesitation. "For years gamers have been saying the Primo controller is too large, feels too big and heavy in their hands, and it can actually cause muscle and joint ache if they hold the thing for too long during an epic gaming session."

"Ah, I remember reading about that in a lengthy Portal forum thread," Ryan said. "Evidently, there's a sizable black market selling the smaller version of the Primo controller we launched in Japan."

"That's interesting," Jack added. "When I was running CI, we helped identify a smaller form-factor controller as something that could help us crack the Japanese market. The average American male's hand is something along the lines of fourteen millimeters larger than the average Japanese male's hand."

"And that's what drove the call for making all standard Primo controllers smaller," Carolyn said. "By chance, a shipment of the Japanese controllers made it out to North American retailers.

Everyone that got their hands on one raved about it. Now everyone else wants one, but they can only get it online from Japan and for a hefty markup. It's the first thing Primo players always point to when they say Hewitt doesn't listen to its customers."

Bob Laurence stepped in and put his hands up. "Let's put this conversation under the lens of our SWOT analysis. Now I know some of you think that SWOT means Stupid Waste of Time or what Ben Gilad has called a Silly Way of Thinking," that laughter in the room broke the tension a bit, "but remember that we're not just here to talk about weaknesses. Strengths and opportunities are critical parts of this equation." He sniffed the air like an eager dog. "I think I even smell a threat in there somewhere."

Jack could feel the temperature in the room drop as the participants were still smiling from Bob's joke. He recognized how deftly his old friend handled the situation and felt grateful to have him on board.

"You've done a terrific job recognizing a weakness," Jack jumped in. "I'd say it's also an opportunity. Play the role of the Market group and ask, 'What strategies does Hewitt need to implement to overcome this weakness and take advantage of the opportunity?'"

"Good point, Jack," Laurence said. "Each element of a Strategic SWOT intersects with other elements: strengths with weaknesses, opportunities with threats. It's within these intersections where companies can find strategic options and actions to leverage their strengths and mitigate their weaknesses." Laurence went on to explain that the Strategic SWOT, also known as The TOWS Matrix, developed by Heinz Weihrich, grew out of the original SWOT framework that is credited to Alberty Humphry, who reportedly developed this tool at the Stanford Research Institute.

Jack felt elated to see Amar begin the conversation anew with the added perspective, followed by Carolyn agreeing with his point. It wasn't just that they quickly put their argument behind them; it was seeing the CFO and the Portal Community Manager putting their fears and egos aside, working together, making their voices heard, and offering their own unique insights. This was precisely the type of open, cross-functional, collaborative environment Jack wanted to foster at Hewitt Games. Jack nearly pinched himself—on top of all that, they were getting real, actionable takeaways.

"Let's leave them to it," Ryan said. "I have the feeling having the chairman and CEO in the room for too long can artificially lower the temperature."

As the debate among the Market team continued, Jack, Ryan, and Laurence stepped into the hall.

"That was terrific, Bob," Ryan said.

"You've still got it, old man." Jack laughed.

"Never lost it," Laurence said, hitching up his pants. "Now if you'll excuse me; it's time for a temperature check on team Apricus."

Back in the CI war room, Jack typed out notes that he would eventually flesh out and add to his CI Playbook.

Jack Turner's CI Playbook
Apply A Strategic Swot:
Finding The Intersections

A Strategic SWOT analysis guides you to identify the positives and negatives inside your organization (Strengths and Weaknesses / S-W) and outside of it in the external environment (Opportunities and Threats / O-T). Where these elements intersect (O-S, O-W, T-S, T-W), organizations will find actionable intelligence.

STRATEGIC SWOT

STRATEGIC SWOT	List Of Internal Strengths	List Of Internal Weaknesses
List Of External Opportunities	Opportunity-Strength (OS) What strategies utilize which strengths to take advantage of the opportunities?	Opportunity-Weakness (OW) What strategies do we need to implement to overcome our weaknesses to take advantage of opportunities?
List Of External Threats	Threat-Strength (TS) What strategies leverage our strengths to blunt threats?	Threat-Weakness (TW) What strategies minimize weaknesses to avoid threats?

17

FIELD OF DREAMS

L IKE A STEAM locomotive laboring to pull out of the station, Hewitt's war game trudged along to start the day. Thanks in large part to Bob Laurence's expert guidance, participants began to find their footing—and their voices. As team members played their roles with greater aplomb, the war game gradually gained speed, and by mid-afternoon, the train was barreling down the tracks.

The momentum in the team rooms carried over to the Insights Hub, and comments began to flow into the portal. Jack noted with great interest that the topic of games continued to pop up. Online and in person, seemingly everyone wanted to know what games would tie into Apricus's and Hewitt's next-generation strategies.

"It's the games, stupid!" Ryan said with enthusiasm when Jack shared this insight.

There wasn't time for a thorough review of the feedback because Jack and Ryan were continually pulled into the team rooms to keep the game focused and moving forward. Time flew by as the Control duo went from team room to war room and back again. Jack shook his head in disbelief when Laurence clasped his shoulder with an update: "It's time to close out Round One. Let's gather the teams to present their findings."

Into the CI war room the teams filed, slightly cramped in the former CEO corner office, but with enough room for all.

"First, let me congratulate you all on a job well done today," Bob Laurence said to the assembled teams. "I've been doing war games for ten years, and I can honestly say I've never seen such progress in a single day, particularly on the *first* day. The way some of you embraced your roles—my goodness! Let's just say Hollywood's Walk of Fame is a few stars short."

Genuine laughs filled the room. Jack noticed nods and smiling exchanges between cross-functional staff members who, he realized, may never have interacted otherwise, let alone have worked together on a critical project.

"And so without further ado, Apricus, you're the away team; you bat first," Laurence said. "Please share with us what you uncovered in your analysis of Hewitt Games."

Per the initial guidance for the war game, each team was to present a boiled-down version of its findings to close out the round in a timely fashion. Specifically, teams were to answer the key questions and goals asked at the outset of the Four Corners analysis. Up first, team Apricus said of Hewitt Games:

1. **Assess your competitor's mindset**: *Complacent to follow its existing model, Hewitt planned to deliver a new generation of Primo console with minor upgrades. Focused solely on its existing competitors, namely Sampson Electronics (which also plans to unveil a new generation console with minor upgrades), Hewitt was caught completely off-guard by our announcement of Sovereign, and our advanced cloud-gaming technology. Major departures in the C-suite and on the board of directors have left the historic*

*company with little in the way of direction and a
mindset it is unfamiliar with: simply survive.*

Uneasy conversations broke out across the room as Jack felt his
own temperature begin to rise.

"Team Hewitt, you will have your chance," Laurence said, his
gravel voice commanding attention. "Let's give team Apricus the
floor, please."

2. **Use analysis to generate insights into the future:** *Just
   as Software as a Service (SaaS) has transformed the
   way companies do business, cloud-gaming will transform the way gamers play games. The days of paying
   for costly hardware every few years are at an end.
   The days of being tethered to your console to play the
   games you love are over. The complete transition will
   take time, but only one company is suited to lead the
   way. We regret to inform you: that company is not
   Hewitt Games. Apricus and Sovereign are the future
   of gaming.*

3. **Help identify the likely strategy your competitor
   will adopt and how successful they may be:** *There are
   no easy answers for Hewitt Games. If the company
   pushes forward with its new console, it will probably
   see a drastic decline in its market share and then be
   faced with playing catchup with Apricus to develop
   its own cloud-gaming service. However, Hewitt owns
   a number of video game development studios, and
   a handful of them have created extremely successful
   game franchises exclusive to the Primo console. One
   clear path forward for Hewitt is to exit the hardware/
   console business altogether and focus solely on software, creating new cross-platform games and leveraging the strength of its existing franchises.*

Another rumble rose in the room. Jack looked at Ryan and saw him raise his eyebrows.

Laurence regained control of the room and introduced team Hewitt. A round of cheers—along with a few playful boos from team Apricus—resonated. Team Hewitt said of Apricus:

> **Assess your competitor's mindset**: *Apricus is a shark that smells blood in the water. There is no denying its cloud-game technology, backed by its global data centers, has the potential to transform the industry. We place heavy emphasis on the word "potential." Yes, Apricus is a shark, but the e-commerce giant is also swimming in the unfamiliar waters of the complex gaming industry. Having trampled just about every e-commerce challenger to come in its path, Apricus is confident and self-assured of a win, perhaps to the point of arrogance. Fortunately for Hewitt Games, Apricus does not know what it doesn't know when it comes to the gaming industry.*

This drew laughs around the room, and even an exciting whoop from Amar Patel. Jack was once again surprised and pleased to see the CFO so genuinely involved in the project.

> **Use analysis to generate insights into the future:** *As we speak, there are an estimated three billion people worldwide who identify as regular gamers, and of those three billion, a full half of them do most of their gaming on PCs. I don't think I need to remind you all how many times over the years PC gaming has been declared dead or dying, thanks in large part to gaming consoles like our Primo. And yet here it remains, stronger than ever. Our point is, in this industry, the birth of new gaming platforms does not equate to the death of old gaming platforms. Rather, we see gamers embracing a mix of old and new. Today, in fact, we know that most gamers enjoy playing across consoles, PC, and mobile. Yes, cloud-gaming is coming, but for the near-term, traditional console gaming isn't going anywhere. We foresee a future where loyal Primo*

customers enjoy playing on a mix of traditional consoles and cloud-gaming platforms.

Help identify the likely strategy your competitor will adopt and how successful they may be: *Apricus says it has the technology. For the time being, we'll accept that Sovereign works as it should, even though no one outside of Apricus has actually seen the cloud-gaming platform in action and proving that it works at scale is a daunting task. Our question then becomes, where are the games? At its big Sovereign unveiling event, Apricus did not introduce a single new AAA game, let alone anything exclusive to its platform. As such, we believe Apricus has put all of its eggs in a first-to-market basket, where it will attempt to gain first-mover advantage and make cloud-gaming synonymous with the Sovereign brand. This is a long-term plan, which we're referring to on the Hewitt team as the "Field of Dreams" strategy. Apricus seems to believe that if they simply build it, gamers will magically emerge out of a cornfield to play Sovereign.*

A raucous cheer arose from the participants as Ryan leaned in. "Once is happenstance, twice is coincidence, three times is a pattern," he said. "It's the games, Jack. The games!"

After Laurence once again calmed the crowd, the speaker continued:

Decades of experience have taught us that big new platforms demand equally big new games to succeed. Platform exclusives drive platform adoption and sales. That's why we believe Apricus' Field of Dreams strategy is highly risky, one that could erase its first-to-market advantages and lead to significant first-mover disadvantages.

∼

After the dust settled on the first day of Hewitt's war game, and long after everyone else had gone home for the night, Jack and Ryan remained in the CI war room, still poring over all of the data.

"When I was a kid, I had this huge baseball card collection," Jack recalled. "I would spend hours upon hours looking at all the stats on the back of cards, marveling at the seasons of some of the greatest of all time. This feels like that."

Ryan looked up from his laptop screen. "I know exactly what you mean; only for me it was Pokémon cards. The art, the abilities, the numbers. I didn't even have to play the game to enjoy the cards."

Jack returned to a file featuring results from the Market team and Insights Hub voters, the same file he'd returned to a dozen times that night.

"Eighty-seven percent market share awarded to Hewitt Games," Jack said, leaning back in his chair. "This is like looking at a sixty-six Willie Mays."

"Or a Surfing Pikachu," Ryan replied, mirroring Jack's lean-back.

"Fifty-two Mickey Mantle."

"Oh, you're going to make me go Rainbow Rare Charizard?"

"I'm not sure what that is, but it sounds magnificent," Jack said.

Ryan laughed. "That it is."

They returned their attention to their respective laptop screens. After a moment of comfortable silence, Jack looked back up. "I can't wait until tomorrow when we find out how our teams will act."

18

COUNTERPUNCH

BOB LAURENCE REFERRED to Day One of the war game as Hewitt's big "Aha!" moment. Day Two, he said, would be the company's first step toward turning insight into action.

"The light bulb turned on," Laurence said to Jack and Ryan in the CI war room as they prepared to begin the second day. "Time to find out what we can do now that we're not fumbling around in the darkness."

The second day's schedule featured two rounds, each round representing a one-year time frame. At the end of the first round, teams would take turns presenting their launch strategies to the entire group. The group would then have the opportunity to challenge each team's proposals, followed by the Market team awarding each team a percentage of market share.

Round two would give the teams the opportunity to counteract the moves made in the first round and to present their final, two-year strategies. The round, the day, and the war game would wrap with a final vote by the Market team.

"Amazing to think this company could be moving in a whole new direction by the end of the day," Jack marveled.

"Give yourself some credit, Jack," Ryan replied. "You started moving Hewitt in a new direction the day you became the CI-Driven CEO."

Jack laughed. "I suppose we started getting everyone into position. But this is it; today is the day, what we've been working so hard towards. Feels like, I don't know, almost like a big trust fall."

"Don't worry," Laurence said, slapping Jack on the back. "We'll catch you."

The momentum from Day One carried over and launched Day Two like a rocket. Participants embraced their roles with vigor; ahead of schedule, both teams were ready to present their proposals.

With the entire group gathered in the CI war room, team Apricus led off, proposing:

- The creation of its own internal game-development studio. The team shared an impressive list of potential creatives who were currently available and promised to invest a sizable sum to make Apricus Studios games must-haves and future drivers of Sovereign adoption.

Licensing a "significant" third-party title to be used during Sovereign beta-testing. Team Apricus conceded a new AAA title was probably impossible for launch but promised that a popular recent Game of the Year—level title would be chosen. The game would then be given as a free gift to all beta-testers after launch. A big-budget promotional push for Sovereign across Apricus's e-commerce platform, with a free thirty-day subscription included with the purchase of any Apricus streaming device, complete with a second free trial that could be gifted to a friend.

"The technology itself, the Sovereign platform, is exclusive," the Apricus team rep concluded. "With its low initial cost and the freedom it will provide to gamers to play where they want and how they want, the technology is what will drive adoption."

Jack gauged the response around the room as tepid at best, and a quick glance at the Insights Portal comments suggested the same.

Team Hewitt countered with a straightforward initial statement: "We confidently propose the launch of our next-generation Primo console as planned, with the unveiling at next year's E3 Expo and shipment in time for the holiday season."

Their proposal included:

- A massive, historic marketing campaign around the two AAA franchise sequels currently in development by Hewitt's internal game studios and set to launch exclusively with the new Primo.

- The development of a monthly paid-subscription service that would give members unlimited access to a rotating catalog of hundreds of games on the new Primo. The new service would be a direct competitor to Sovereign's subscription offering and serve as the precursor for Hewitt's eventual transition to cloud-gaming.

- The strategic acquisition of one of the world's biggest games publishers. Team Hewitt provided a short-list of targets, with Pixel Productions at the top.

After a stunned silence, the room erupted.

Hewitt Games enjoyed a long, strong history with Pixel Productions, and Jack knew many of the top executives at the privately held company. It ranked as the eighth-largest publisher in terms of revenue and was the proud owner of three beloved and acclaimed game franchises—titles that were always among Primo's top sellers.

"It's a smart pick," Ryan affirmed, leaning in to be heard over the clamor. "What would it take? Realistic ballpark number?"

"Well, we know that the biggest publisher in the world, Atomic Games, took a run at Pixel a little over a year ago," Jack replied. "I had solid intel that they turned down two billion, but it was supposedly less about the money and more about it being a bad fit culturally."

Ryan nodded and sat back as Bob Laurence brought order to the room. The restoration of calm was brief as Laurence commenced the challenge period of the round. There were a handful of questions regarding team Apricus's proposal, but the deluge fell on team Hewitt and the targeted acquisition of Pixel Productions.

CFO Amar Patel was instrumental in the discussions, providing a detailed look into Hewitt's financial position.

"I'd recommend opening a new asset-based credit facility to improve liquidity," Patel proposed, "but otherwise we're well-positioned for a sizable strategic acquisition."

A debate ensued about whether the money would be better spent acquiring one of the handful of small companies working on their own cloud-gaming technology. Ultimately, CMO Amanda Givens' voice rose above the fray and garnered consensus.

"The gaming world, the financial world, and most importantly our loyal customers have been awaiting Hewitt's response to Sovereign for months," she said. "The acquisition of some startup cloud-gaming company no one has ever heard of? That's not a response; that's a concession that Apricus was right all along. An enthusiastic embrace of second place. I can already see the memes."

A much-needed laugh eased the tension. Amanda continued, "Let's not just respond; let's break our silence with a knockout of a counter-punch. Let's make a major acquisition and announce that Hewitt Games is now the exclusive home of the best games in the world."

The room erupted with applause that Bob Laurence allowed to run long. When calm returned, after listening intently throughout the challenge period, Jack weighed in.

"I think we can all agree that our industry is transitioning into a truly player-centric era," he said. "Each progressive console generation, it's less about the devices, and more about the players. And if there is one thing players want, it's to play the best games from the industry's most talented creators. It's that simple. So, if we have the opportunity to bring more of the best games and more of the most talented creators to Hewitt Games, we should do it. Let's throw that haymaker counter punch."

"Agreed," Ryan said. He patted his pockets in an exaggerated fashion. "Anyone see where I put my checkbook?"

"Hey!" Bob Laurence exclaimed over the laughter. "Don't forget we've got votes to cast and there's another round to play. If this was year one, I can't wait to see what Hewitt has in store for year two!"

~

After the dust settled on year-two moves, countermoves, and debate, and the final votes were cast, Hewitt Games drew the curtain on its first business war game. Jack Turner and his team held the actionable outcomes Bob Laurence promised, and so much more.

"Ninety-two percent market share for Hewitt Games," Jack said, shaking his head in disbelief as he threw his arm over Sofia's shoulder. "Ninety-two!"

Sofia had stayed up late, greeting Jack with a glass of champagne and enthusiastic questions. "You sure no one sandbagged the Apricus proposal? Bob Laurence can be intimidating for an old guy."

"Sorry, you're in the 'no bad jokes zone' tonight," Jack replied. "Team Hewitt crushed a home run today. And not just team Hewitt, all of Hewitt Games. The primary and secondary research compiled by CI and Marketing, collaborating like never before. The new two-way information portal, giving the entire company a robust single point to learn about and share intelligence. The cross-functional teams, working together with honesty, passion, and respect to produce powerful, actionable intelligence."

"The new CEO," Sofia jumped in, "who envisioned this CI one-voice transformation ages ago, and who, under ridiculous circumstances, managed to pull off a remarkable turnaround."

"Correction: managed to pull off the first step in what could become a remarkable turnaround," Jack said. "Though I do appreciate the kind words and I love that you stayed up so late to greet me." He sighed and looked at his watch. "But I better get to bed. Today, we finally figured out how to best respond to Apricus. Tomorrow, the work begins to put the plan into practice."

19

LOST AND FOUND

WHEN JACK PULLED into Hewitt's parking garage well before sunrise the next morning, he found someone other than Ryan Corbin had beat him into the office. That is, unless Ryan swapped out his secret agent supercar for a Volvo.

On the forty-second floor, Jack followed the dim light down the hall to Amar Patel's office and found the CFO tapping away at his keyboard. Intently focused on his monitor, Amar didn't notice Jack lean in, and nearly jumped out of his seat when Jack said, "Morning!"

"Forgive me," Amar said, breathing deep. "I wasn't expecting to see anyone at this hour."

"No, my apologies. I should have rapped on the door before popping in like that," Jack replied. "Ryan Corbin is typically the only one to beat me into the office; what brings you here so early?"

Jack could see Amar didn't look like his usual calm, cool self. The hour and being startled like that were the obvious reasons, but Jack sensed it might be something else.

"Oh, uh, well," Amar stammered. "I wasn't expecting ... wanted to finish this for you before...."

Jack stepped closer. "Amar, is everything okay?"

Amar took a deep breath, straightened his collar, and regained most of his composure. He tapped his keyboard and a nearby printer whirred to life. Amar stood, grabbed the document when it emerged, and handed it to Jack.

"I apologize that I've not yet completed compiling the specific metrics you requested to determine return on competitive intelligence," he said. "You said it was a top priority, and I should have completed the project sooner."

"Don't sweat it, Amar," Jack answered. "We've all had our hands full. I know how hard you've been working."

"I've developed a greater understanding of the CI function and its benefits over the past few months, and I believe this framework will be a useful tool for you going forward. Once you understand the metrics to measure based on input from your stakeholder, and then you actually assess the impact of those metrics, again based on what the stakeholder believes to be the value or assumptions you make, and you report out those successes, you'll be able to show value. But you also need the blessing of someone in finance and it would be important to build a CI-friendly culture along the way."

"Amar, this is perfect," Jack said. "I wasn't sure you would wrap your head around perspective over precision when it comes to qualitative benefits, but you nailed it. This will be a terrific guide going forward. Can't wait to use it to determine ROCI for the war game and share with Julie to apply for all future CI projects. I don't ever want the CI function to be viewed as an expense or overhead again; it should be a huge asset on our balance sheet, not a liability!"

As Jack looked over the framework, Amar went back around his desk, tapped keys to print another document. This one he signed before handing it to Jack.

"And what's this?" Jack asked. He looked up and noticed the cool demeanor crumbling again.

"It's my letter of resignation," Amar admitted. "I'm sorry, Jack; it was me who spoke to Cliff Carlton. I was the leak."

ROCI®: A FRAMEWORK FOR RETURN ON CI

Obtain input from stakeholders throughout the intelligence process on perceived value of deliverables

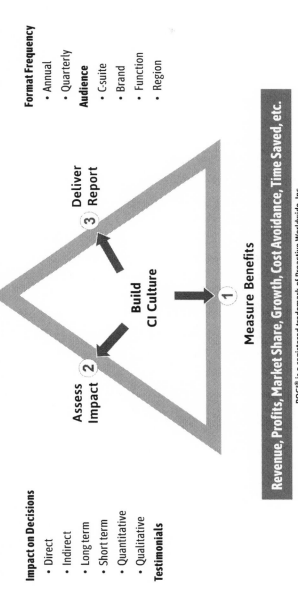

Format Frequency
- Annual
- Quarterly

Audience
- C-suite
- Brand
- Function
- Region

Deliver Report

3

Build CI Culture

1

Assess Impact

2

Measure Benefits

Revenue, Profits, Market Share, Growth, Cost Avoidance, Time Saved, etc.

ROCI® is a registered trademark of Proactive Worldwide, Inc.

Impact on Decisions
- Direct
- Indirect
- Long term
- Short term
- Quantitative
- Qualitative

Testimonials

∼

The rising sun poked between buildings, casting blocks of warm orange light through the window in Jack's office.

"I don't know all the details, how they got in touch, but Fei Hong was the first to speak with Carlton's producer," Amar recalled, standing at the window with his hands in his pockets, his white shirt looking sherbet-colored in the light. "He evidently asked if there was anyone else who could corroborate her story, and she sent him to me. Before I knew it, I was speaking with Cliff Carlton himself."

Jack recalled the first day of the war game, seeing Amar unance characteristically lose his cool when a colleague was critical of Hewitt Games. He recognized now it was Amar's own guilt that had caused the reaction.

"Was there an end-game here?" Jack asked. "What were you hoping to accomplish?"

"You have to understand," Amar explained, turning around, "we suspected Ryan Corbin was up to no good, a vulture waiting to swoop in to feast on the carcass of Hewitt Games. We honestly believed he named you as CEO in an effort to expedite the company's demise."

"Ouch," Jack winced.

"I'm sorry, truly."

"No, I get it. If I'm being perfectly honest, I had my own doubts about Ryan Corbin and wondered if he was propping me up to be his fall guy."

"Thank you for sharing that," Amar said, turning back to the window. "You asked why? Well we were hoping the negative press would diminish Ryan's power over the board, force their hand to—"

"Find a replacement for the unqualified interim CEO; I get it." Jack sighed.

"Fei saw it first, the positive impact you were having, the good work Ryan was doing. She resigned in shame. I planned to join her, but she convinced me my position was too important to the transition. So, like a coward, I stayed."

Jack stood, and began pacing behind his desk.

"For what it's worth, I finally get it," Amar said. "A CI-supportive culture. The CI war game, involving the entire company, the Insights Hub, witnessing the transformation you've preached about actually coming to life. And getting real, intelligence-based, actionable outcomes out of it all—well done, Jack. Well done."

Jack stopped pacing, and made his decision. "Fei was right about one thing: you're too important to lose," he said, tearing up Amar's letter. "I refuse your resignation, and this is not up for debate. Just promise me one thing?"

Amar shook his head, eyes wide and glassy, "I—I, of course anything."

"Cliff Carlton ever calls you again, tell him Jack Turner said he's a buffoon."

~

Jack set up shop in Andy Barrows' office, hoping to catch his friend first thing. While he waited, the pictures and keepsakes lining the walls and shelves sparked nostalgic memories.

College—a lifetime and a few inches' worth of floppy hair ago. Andy's destination wedding in Waikiki, the best vacation Jack and Sofia had ever had. An awkward photo of new recruits Andy and Jack standing beside Howard Hewitt himself, the legend. A picture of Keri and Cody when they were toddlers, grinning ear to ear and covered head to toe with wet mud. Jack laughed, snapped a picture with his phone and texted the image to his kids.

"I know I framed a copy of that exact pic and gave it to you at some point," Andy said, standing in the doorway.

"It hangs in my upstairs hall," Jack answered. "But seeing it here reminded me that I need to remember to reach out to Cody more often."

"Holiday break soon, let's all get something on the books, maybe catch a Blackhawks game when he's home."

"Deal," Jack said.

Andy hung his coat and opened his laptop bag. "To what do I owe the honor at this early hour?"

"Fei Hong," Jack said. "What's the status of our separation agreement with her?"

"The mysterious case of the disappearing executive. Legal was giving it one final pass, should go out today for signature. Why? What's up?"

"Good, cancel it, and work your magic to get her on the phone," Jack said. "Tell her I spoke with Amar Patel, I know what happened, and I refuse to accept her resignation. This company needs its COO back."

20

PHOENIX

Prior to Hewitt's "aha" moment, the in-development, next-generation Primo console had felt like an albatross around the company's neck. Post-CI war game, it became a blessing, and it even earned itself a new internal code name: Project Phoenix.

With all systems now set firmly to go on the production of the new hardware, Jack felt reinvigorated by the clear target goal in Hewitt's sights: create the best Primo ever and have it ready for launch in time for the next holiday season, roughly one year from now.

That also meant a second, much tighter deadline: Project Phoenix's unveiling at the Electronics Entertainment Expo in six months.

Oh, and Jack also had to continue to lead the company's transition to a CI-supportive culture, convince the eighth largest publisher of games in the world that they should sell, and create a new subscription games service for Primo that would put anything Apricus offered to shame.

With so much to do, Jack begrudgingly began to finally address one of his greatest professional weaknesses: delegation. It was while Jack was working on team assignments that an alert on the Insights Hub caught his attention. He clicked the link and found the first in a planned series of stories from marketing on the success of the CI war game. This particular article focused on Carolyn Copley, the Portal Community Manager who stared down Amar Patel and brought attention to Hewitt's oversized Primo controllers:

> We asked for your honest thoughts and opinions, and Carolyn delivered in a major way, providing much-needed insight from Primo's loyal fans. Thanks to her efforts, we realize the controllers on our next generation Primo need a major design overhaul. And they'll get one ... with Carolyn's assistance! She'll assist the design team as they rework Primo's most important accessory to help ensure the voice of our customers is heard loud and clear. Actionable intelligence from internal sources? That's real CI at work!

Words of congratulations and support began popping into the article's comment section before Jack was done reading. He smiled and added his own thumbs-up emoji to the rapidly growing list, marveling as the comments continued to pour in.

A rap on the door. Ryan Corbin, open laptop in hand, and asked, "Are you seeing this, the story on Carolyn Copley?"

"Just read it," Jack said. "So nice!"

Ryan walked in and sat down. "Nice? Nice doesn't even begin to cover it. Do you have any idea what this means?"

Jack laughed. "That the design team is going to have their hands full with Carolyn?"

Ryan clicked away on his laptop before turning the screen, revealing a slide that read:

1. Have at least one C-suite champion

2. Educate people regularly on what CI is and isn't

3. Brand and internally market the research unit

4. Know and profile the research function's campaigns

5. Encourage and recognize staff contributions

6. Regularly share successes / impact

"Look at this list, the one we brainstormed months ago when I asked you what it would take to create a CI-supportive culture." Ryan slapped a hand on top of his head. "We're checking nearly every box!"

The memory of the night in the luxury box at the United Center for the Bulls game came back bright and vivid. Jack felt the same shot of enthusiasm now as he had felt then.

Ryan stood and threw his arms up as if he had just scored a goal. "It means it's working, Jack. It's really working!"

~

There were plenty of other knocks on Jack's office door that day, including Fei Hong's.

With her hat and long coat on and purse in hand, the COO looked out of place, like a visitor stopping by to ask for directions.

"Andy Barrows called..."

Jack invited her in and they sat, started an awkward chat about the Chicago weather before Fei interjected with, "Jack, I'm so sorry. So deeply, sincerely sorry. I've done some dumb things in my life that I'm not proud of, but never anything that comes remotely close to this level of shameful stupidity. Cliff Carlton's producer called me out of the blue, and I just started babbling like—"

"Woah, woah, woah," Jack interrupted, holding up his hands. "Fei, it's okay, really." He took a deep breath. "I'll say the same thing to you that I said to Amar: I get it. I wish it hadn't happened, and I wish I had those two minutes of my life back where I had to listen to that blowhard throw me under the bus, but I get it. I understand why."

"It's no excuse," Fei insisted, dropping her head.

"I also told Amar that he's too important to lose, and I refused to accept his resignation. The same goes for you, Fei. You are a terrific COO, and this company needs you now more than ever."

She looked up. "I—I don't know what to say."

Jack popped up and grabbed his laptop from his desk, clicked through to find what he was looking for. He brought it around so Fei could see. It was a diagram of the teams Jack created to tackle Hewitt's strategy. Fei's name featured prominently, leading the team that would manage the company's critical E3 presentation.

"Say you'll get started on this project ASAP," Jack said. "No one knows events and logistics as you do, and it's not a stretch to say we need this to be our greatest E3 presentation ever."

Fei fought back tears, took a deep breath, and stood up. She removed her hat and coat and draped it over her arm.

"If it's okay with you, boss, I'll get started immediately," she said, extending her hand.

Jack gave it a firm shake. "Let's get to work."

21

SPOTLIGHT

STANDING BACKSTAGE AT the Los Angeles Convention Center, Jack recalled the strange, out-of-touch phenomenon during the Covid lockdown that had become popularly known as Blursday, when every day blurred into the next and Father Time seemed to run his clock on rocket fuel.

As he awaited his cue to address the raucous capacity crowd for Hewitt's E3 conference presentation, Jack realized the time warp he had entered six months ago made Covid Blursdays look stagnant.

"You okay?" Ryan Corbin asked, placing a steady hand on Jack's shoulder. "You crushed it in rehearsal. Don't worry; we've got this."

"No, I'm good," Jack assured him, shaking the cobwebs. "Great, actually. I just can't believe we're standing here, about to do this. Seems like yesterday, hell, *this morning*, when I walked into Gibson's steakhouse and found you waiting to surprise me. All those days and weeks and months between then and now"—he snapped his fingers— "gone in a snap."

"Agreed," Ryan laughed. "I don't know where the time went, but I do know beyond a shadow of a doubt that it was well spent."

Jack heard the master of ceremonies begin their introduction and saw the curtain start to rise as the audience cheered.

"Ready?" Ryan asked.

Jack nodded. "Let's make Howard Hewitt proud."

Ryan expressed, "Having a CI-driven CEO leading this company sure makes me proud."

∼

The crowd shook the building and social media erupted with adulation, but Jack knew they'd really hit a home run with their presentation when reviews of Hewitt's E3 presentation from the notoriously snarky gaming press rolled in, gushing with genuine praise.

The list of major announcements made Hewitt the unanimous E3 conference winner:

- The fastest, most powerful Primo console ever, Phoenix, with a new re-designed controller built to gamer specifications and hitting store shelves in mid-November with an MSRP below the launch price of the last Primo

- Spectacular, Primo-exclusive launch titles, including sequels to some of the most popular franchises in gaming from Hewitt Game Studios

- Primo Pass, the new subscription game service that would give clients unlimited access to an initial library of more than one-hundred titles for just eight dollars a month

- And the surprise, showstopper announcement: the official acquisition of Pixel Productions, bringing a murderers' row of beloved gaming franchises exclusively to Hewitt's PrimoPreorders opened online at select retail partners the moment the show ended, and just as quickly as they appeared, they disappeared, completely sold out.

Hewitt's ticker saw a surge it hadn't seen since its initial IPO decades prior, pushing the stock price to finally get in line with the company's strong fundamental valuation.

That night, as Jack, his family and friends, and the entire company celebrated at its post-conference party, Cliff Carlton adjusted his outlook for Hewitt Games on live TV, begrudgingly shifting from "sell" to "hold."

"But let's not go counting our chickens before they hatch," Carlton warned. "We still haven't heard how Apricus will respond."

That response came the very next day, with Apricus announcing the opening of the first beta-test for Sovereign.

As Hewitt predicted in its CI war game, a major AAA title would be used during testing—just not a new or exclusive game. Sign-ups filled quickly and there appeared to be genuine interest, even among Primo loyalists. But as media outlets, analysts, and gamers noted, the announcement did nothing to slow the momentum behind Hewitt Games and the excitement for the new Primo. Despite the poor initial diagnosis after Sovereign's initial announcement, console gaming remained alive and well.

Somewhere, Ryan Corbin grinned, telling Jack Turner, "It's the games, stupid!"

EPILOGUE

BOSTON BLOOMED WITH early summer buds, filling the air with a soft fragrance. Jack breathed it in deep when he stepped out of his car, relishing the sweetness before exhaling the stale air of the road from his lungs.

"Oh, that feels good," Sofia enthused, stepping out on the passenger side with a long stretch. "Now let's go get our baby boy!"

Somehow, Cody's dorm room seemed even smaller than when Jack had first stepped foot in it nearly a year before. It must have been his son, who, standing in the middle of the room surrounded by boxes, looked like he had put on ten pounds of muscle.

After hugging his mother, Cody exulted, "Congratulations, mister chief executive," and gave his father a crushing hug. "How does it feel to ditch the temporary title?"

"Oof," Jack replied. "Go easy on your old man! It feels amazing. I honestly still can't believe it. This past year, just mind-blowing."

"Well, if the response to Hewitt's E3 from my friends is any indicator, it was well deserved," Cody said. "Everybody's talking about the new Primo."

"Good to hear," Jack said as his phone rang once, stopped, followed by a second call a moment later.

"Andy, did I ever tell you just how small my son's dorm room is?"

"Sorry to bother you, Jack, but I wanted to give you a heads-up," Andy said. "The strategic early warning system your team set up got a hit on a potential new market entrant. New tech focused on creating a blockchain-based gaming platform."

"Huh," Jack said. "That's one interesting way to take crypto mainstream. Well, if the early warning system picked up on it, it's definitely worth a close look. I don't ever want our competitors to surprise us again. Thanks for the heads-up. Talk soon."

"Oh no, not again," Cody said.

"It's not another black dawn, is it Jack?" Sofia asked. "Please don't tell me you have to jump on a plane."

Jack laughed as he ended the call. "It's 'black swan,' and no, I do not have to jump on a plane. We're tracking indicators that tell us which scenario about the future is most plausible. I'll explain it to you later. Bottom line, it's nothing to worry about and nothing we can't handle. Hewitt Games is a CI company now."

APPENDIX

ACKNOWLEDGMENTS

THIS BOOK REFLECTS our experience over three decades of intelligence work in servicing some of the largest and most respected companies in the world. We thank all of the hundreds of companies and thousands of individual clients we have had the pleasure of learning from and working with across the globe and in so many core industries. We also thank the Strategic and Competitive Intelligence Professionals (SCIP) for a long-standing partnership and ongoing collaboration to put CI more on center stage as being critical to any company's success.

We would especially like to thank Michael Sharkey, our editor, for his countless interactions and contributions, not only to our first book in 2011, *New Directions: A Competitive Intelligence Tale*, but for his collaboration with us to craft this story. Special thanks also go to Henry DeVries of Indie Books International, our editor and publisher, for the positive encouragement and consistent guidance that allowed us to turn our manuscript into a finished product. And finally, thank you to all of the team members at our firm, Proactive Worldwide, who provide outstanding service and consistently deliver CI excellence to our clients every day—you're the best!

ABOUT THE AUTHORS

GARY D. MAAG has been a leader in the business research community with over thirty years dedicated specifically to competitive intelligence. He has assisted dozens of Fortune 500 companies in high-profile competitive intelligence engagements. In 2006, the Society of Competitive Intelligence Professionals (SCIP) awarded Maag the Catalyst Award for his contributions to the profession. He was the founder of the graduate-level CI program at Dominican University and the co-founder and CEO of Proactive Worldwide, Inc. For speaking information and bulk copies of this book, please contact Gary at garym@proactiveworldwide.com.

DAVID J. KALINOWSKI is a CI veteran with more than thirty years of expertise in the CI field and co-founder and president of Proactive Worldwide, Inc. Kalinowski has directed CI research and analysis for hundreds of domestic and international corporations, assisted C-suite leaders in building their in-house intelligence capability, and informed numerous advisory and executive boards on highly sensitive CI strategy development, war-gaming, and training initiatives. In 2005, Kalinowski won SCIP's Catalyst Award, and once served on the SCIP Board of Directors as well as the Treasurer and a Director of the Board at the Society of Insurance Research. For speaking information and bulk copies of this book, please contact David at davidk@proactiveworldwide.com.

GO DEEPER IN YOUR COMPETITIVE INTELLIGENCE PROFESSIONAL DEVELOPMENT

CI Blueprint℠

The on-demand CI Blueprint℠ course will help you increase the impact you have at your company and improve the quality of what you produce. We designed this training to reduce your learning time while providing guidance on how you can best add value to your company. A variety of course techniques will get you engaged and teach you to absorb, retain, and apply the key takeaways.

www.cilearninglab.com